MY HANDMADE WEDDING

First published in 2016

Search Press Limited
Wellwood, North Farm Road,
Tunbridge Wells, Kent TN2 3DR

Suppliers

If you have difficulty in obtaining any of the materials and
equipment mentioned in this book, then please visit the
Search Press website for details of suppliers:
www.searchpress.com

Printed in China

Dedication

First, I would like to dedicate this book
to my husband Dave, who supported
me tremendously and accomplished
everything I couldn't throughout
our wedding journey. He put a lot of
trust in me to make our day enjoyable
and special and I thank him for his
continued belief in my crazy ideas.
I also feel this book should be dedicated
to my parents, Linda and John Mercer.
They have always encouraged me in my
crafty and arty abilities and have always
seen the potential in my ideas. The
support has always been beyond what
any daughter could ask for. There are
not many parents who would take bossy
orders from their youngest and go on
to make 300 metres of bunting for her
wedding. Thank you also for allowing
me and Dave to share the date of your
wedding forty-four years later.

MY HANDMADE WEDDING

Marrianne Mercer

SEARCH PRESS

CONTENTS

INTRODUCTION

As Dave and I approached four years together, I started to realise that perhaps this was going to be for the long term. With that in mind, I started to take note of ideas that I liked from our friends' weddings and parties – like many people in our early thirties, we seemed to be surrounded by friends tying the knot. From the offset of our engagement I knew I wanted to create a 'handmade', crafty wedding.

I had joined Search Press as one of their in-house graphic designers a few years before this. Not only was I being bombarded by beautiful weddings in my personal life, but also stunning crafts in my work life. It made me really think about how the crafts I was surrounded by each day could be adapted for a wedding celebration that was a bit different to those that we had been to as guests.

As a designer, I like to take elements of inspiration from others and adapt them into something unique that pleases my eye and, perhaps, my pocket! You will find, as I have, that attending lots of different weddings shows you lots of different ways of doing things, which can help you to focus your likes and dislikes. One wedding in particular influenced me and made me realise that actually, the big, expensive, picturesque hotel or stately mansion wedding wasn't for me. It was the wedding of Richard and Anna, some close friends of ours. They had a wonderfully relaxed wedding ceremony in a beautiful local registry office followed by a garden reception at a relative's house. They had ample garden space and woodland, with a marquee next to the house. In the weeks leading up to the wedding, a few of us were asked to each make 10m (33ft) of bunting in pastel colours. This was used to decorate the inside of the marquee. I also popped by the day before with a few others to help make cakes for the reception party and set up the garden with decorations. It was wonderful to see it all come together and feel that we had a part in making it happen for them. On the day itself there was no formal three-course wedding breakfast. Instead they served their guests a cream tea, followed later by a delicious hog roast and salad buffet, accompanied by big ice-filled buckets full of drinks. A friend's band played in the evening, before they switched to an iPod played over the speakers. It was so original, relaxed and personal and one of the first DIY weddings I had come across. I loved it!

I had a conversation with Anna the day before her wedding, which heavily influenced my own. While busily making her own beautiful flower decorations she explained that at the start of her planning, she had looked into making paper flowers, to save on the cost of professional floristry fees, but decided they would take too long... This was the spark that lit my creative fire!

So I knew I wanted a handmade celebration, but where to hold it? I liked the idea of decorating a village hall. It is a blank canvas to which almost any design can be applied, and it's a budget-friendly option compared to venues such as stately homes and gardens. Living in Kent, we are surrounded by local villages that have held onto their Kentish roots and traditions. The village of Leigh in particular stood out for me. I went to pre-school and primary school there, and attended the little village church for many of the year-round services.

Dave and I visited the village hall quite early on and I fell in love with its photo-friendly high ceilings and huge church-like windows straight away. We were shown around by the caretaker who chatted away to us, telling us how his daughter had used it as a wedding reception venue. He showed us all the furniture that was included and told us about the options for catering.

We were keen to be thorough, so we visited a few other places and made lists of pros and cons for each venue, considering size, costs, any extras that were included in the package and how guests would travel between venues. But after visiting and meeting the friendly congregation at St Mary's Church in Leigh, we decided that a church wedding, with all the extras – bells, organist and flying union flags – followed by a reception in the village hall just two minutes' walk down the road, was exactly what we wanted. One of the few dates they had available was my parents' wedding date, forty-four years before, so in my eyes it was meant to be.

It's a great idea to create a DIY wedding – I can't recommend it highly enough. Not only is it likely to save you some money, it gets your imagination and creativity flowing, which will make your wedding much more personal and heart-felt. Whether you go all out and create everything you can, or just pick and choose a few handmade highlights, it will make a big difference to your day. DIY weddings can also have the benefit of softening the blow for the groom. If, like mine, your groom is nauseous at the thought of the huge costs involved or dreads the idea of a long-winded formal day of smiling until his face cracks, a simpler, more relaxed DIY day may be the solution. It can be easy to achieve a relaxed, personal, intimate and enjoyable day that doesn't break the bank!

Designing and making the amount that I did for our wedding gave me an amazing sense of achievement and satisfaction. I know from having helped Anna with her wedding that when you ask friends and family to help create your day, they too share in that same feeling of success when it all comes together, so don't be afraid to ask them for help. Creating as much as I did isn't for everyone. It is very time-consuming and the only way I achieved it all in eight months was by being super organised, having a very tolerant fiancé and relying on plenty of support from our friends and family. Even if you make just a few items, it helps to personalise your day, will save you some cash to spend in other areas and may give you and your guests something to cherish on and after the big day.

The most important advice I can give you before you embark on a handmade wedding, no matter how big or small, is to be **SUPER ORGANISED**. You can never do enough **RESEARCH**. Make **LISTS** at every stage of the process: to-do lists, done lists, tomorrow lists and suppliers' lists. Lists equal organisation, which will result in a smooth, successful day.

Good luck and enjoy the rollercoaster!

PLANNING YOUR WEDDING

So you're engaged: congratulations! But what now? Planning your big day is a time-consuming and emotional journey in which you start to focus on who you are as a couple, and the sort of day you want to remember for the rest of your lives. Make it simple by starting with a few questions…

1 Where do you want to get married?

2 What time of year would you like to get married? Do you have a special date in mind?

3 Religious service or civil ceremony?

4 What's your budget?

5 How many people do you want to share your day?

6 What theme or look would you both like?

7 What colour or colours would you like?

January	February	March	April	May
1	1	1 Suit fitting 1	1	1
2	2	2	2	2
	3	3	3	3
	4	4	4 Veil	4 Su
	5	5	5 Hair flower	5
	6	6	6	6
7	7	7	7	7
8	8	8	8	8
9 Candle making	9	9	9	9
10		10	10 Corsages	10
11		11	11	11
12		12	12	13
13		13	13	1
14		14	14 Bouquets	1
15		15	15	
16 Bunting		16	16	
17		17	17	
18		18	18	
19		19	19	
20		20	20 Hair trial	
21		21	21	
22		22	22	
23		23	23	
24 Meet caterer		24	24	
25 Invitations		25	25	
26 Hire hall	26	26	26	
27	27 Candle making	27	27	
28	28	28	28	
29		29	29	
30		30 Order rings	30	
31		31		

June	July	August	September	October	November	December
1	1	1 Set up day	1	1	1	1
2	2	2 Wedding day	2	2	2	2
3	3	3 Honeymoon!	3	3	3	3
4	4	4	4	4	4	4
5 Dress fitting	5	5	5	5	5	5
6	6	6	6	6	6	6
7	7	7	7	7	7	7
8 Decoupage	8	8	8	8	8	8
9	9	9	9	9	9	9
10	10	10	10	10	10	10
11	11	11	11	11	11	11
12	12	12	12	12	12	12
13 Lanterns	13 Chalkboard	13	13	13	13	13
14	14	14	14	14	14	14
15	15	15	15	15	15	15
16	16	16	16	16	16	16
17	17	17	17	17	17	17
18	18	18	18	18	18	18
19	19	19	19	19	19	19
20	20	20	20	20	20	20
21	21	21	21	21	21	21
22	22	22	22	22	22	22
23 Cake trial	23 Print signage	23	23	23	23	23
24	24 Dress fitting	24	24	24	24	24
25	25	25	25	25	25	25
26	26	26	26	26	26	26
27	27 Bake cakes	27	27	27	27	27
28	28 Ice cakes	28	28	28	28	28
29	29 Decorate cakes	29	29	29	29	29
30	30 Rehearsal	30	30	30	30	30
	31 Collect dress	31		31		

n Flowers

CHOOSING A VENUE

The most important things to do first are to draw up a headcount and work out your budget: you need to know how many guests you would like to invite in order to choose a venue that will not only accommodate the numbers but also be affordable. It's important to be realistic at this stage, or you may have to make difficult decisions or cut your guest numbers later on if you choose a venue that is unsuitable.

Get a rough idea

If you're feeling a bit overwhelmed by the range of possibilities available to you, take some time with your fiancé and brainstorm a list of things you both want from your wedding. Inevitably, your big day will be unlikely to include all of these things, but thinking about it up front can help you to focus your ideas and work out which of your ideas are 'must-haves' and which are just 'nice-to-haves'. For example, if you've always pictured a religious ceremony followed by a rustic barn reception and he wants a more formal civil ceremony, now is the time to work out where you need to compromise, and how you can mesh your ideas together.

It's also worth considering the time of year that you want, as this will affect almost every other aspect of your wedding, and can make a huge difference to the cost. Winter weddings are often cheaper as they are out of peak season. However, think about the implications the weather may have. You don't want to ruin your outfit by walking too far in the snow, you'll need to wrap up warm for outdoor photographs, and you might also want to consider that older buildings may be less efficient at keeping the heat in. Equally, in summer you won't want to get too hot in a big, heavy dress and a tiny cramped venue.

> **Other important things to budget for...**
> - Wedding rings
> - Bride's dress
> - Groom's suit
> - Outfits for bridesmaids, groomsmen, ushers, page boys and flower girls
> - Flowers
> - Catering
> - Wedding cake
> - Entertainment
> - Venue decorations
> - Favours
> - Wedding stationery
> - Honeymoon

We chose St Mary's Church in Leigh, Kent (see opposite) followed by a reception in the village hall. It was a two-minute walk for our guests from one place to the other and was also close to a pub for guests who arrived early. It also worked out to be the most affordable route to take.

Do your research

I cannot stress how important this is. Check out wedding blogs and websites that showcase real weddings and search online to find buildings, venues and spaces that are available to hire. Jot down the prices, making a note of exactly what these prices include. Roughly work out how the price would affect the rest of your budget, so that you can start to rule out places that are too expensive and work out the key areas on which you are willing to spend more. There are lots of different routes you can go down with both the ceremony and reception, and each of them will require different amounts of handmade decoration. Try to create a shortlist of potential venues.

We researched many local wedding venues for civil marriages. Some of the most beautiful locations charge prices that reflect this and were completely out of our budget. You must also factor in registrar fees as these are an additional cost on top of the venue hire. Venues that can host the ceremony and reception might do discounts if you hold both in one place, but you must check how much decoration you can do yourself as many do not welcome handmade weddings.

We found it easier to visit the venues that we had shortlisted based on our online research and then write a list of pros and cons for each place, including factors such as size, costs, any extras in the package, travel between the ceremony to the reception venue and corkage fees. Doing this also helped us to decide what was important.

Keep it local

If you can, check out as many local venues as possible. Having a local venue was incredibly helpful to me during the creative process as it meant I could easily visit to check the sizes of the rooms and where the decorations would fit; it allows the extra level of control that you need for a handmade wedding. Going local also means that the logistics of set-up day are simple: we had several carloads of paper flowers to transport for the church and reception, and another trip just for the cake.

TIP:
GET INVOLVED
Go and look around venues, meet vicars, talk to the locals and get a feel for the places you have shortlisted.

TIP:
A CLOSE CALL
Being a short journey from the venue helped us out on a number of occasions: when I showed my parents the plan for the bunting at our reception, they could see a better way of displaying it. A quick five-minute drive to the venue enabled us to re-measure and draw up a new and better-looking plan. Easy!

CHOOSING A THEME

Once you have a venue, next comes inspiration. Again, do your research. Find items, images, photographs and flowers – anything that appeals to you both – and collect them in a box or create a moodboard.

Getting inspiration

Visiting wedding or country fairs can give you great ideas to turn into little craft projects. Do your research before you go: many suppliers offer discounts for deals done at fairs – but do make sure you're getting the best possible value. Also look for wedding inspiration online. Websites such as Pinterest are excellent as they not only inspire you and allow you to collect and organise your ideas, but often supply the step-by-step instructions or the contact details of the original supplier or crafter.

Time of year

The theme you choose is likely to be heavily influenced by the time of year you get married. In the spring months, people traditionally choose light, soft floral themes; summer weddings are often brighter and more colourful, while winter themes are bolder and richer in colour, or sparkly and simple with ice and snow themes of silver, white and blue. Of course, there's nothing to stop you having any colour you like at any time of year, but think carefully about the flowers you might want, and check their year-round availability.

Choosing a colour scheme

Whether you decide to go for a vintage, country, contemporary, retro or chic theme, you will need a colour scheme and you will need to stick to it. Get some colour inspiration online: searching for a wedding colour palette will bring up sets of colour swatches that complement each other. If you already have an idea of what your main colour might be, spend some time thinking about what colours complement this – you might find that you are drawn to combinations you would never have considered before.

I found two flower bouquet images that I loved, both very different in colour. One was a variety of pastel colours; the other was a mix of summer brights. Both would have looked beautiful, but in the end, the decision came down to which we felt was more 'me', even if we felt it was less traditionally 'weddingy' – so we opted for the bright summer colour palette.

MEASURING UP

In order to know how much of everything to make or buy, you need to go and thoroughly measure both the ceremony and the reception venues. This is especially key if you are hiring a blank room, such as a village hall, as it will require more creative vision. Other hired spaces, such as hotels, often have a layout that they know works for large parties, so you can use that to plan what you need to make. Getting an accurate set of measurements early on will make the rest of the planning easy: you will need to work out how all the large elements, such as tables, chairs and the dance floor will fit, but also how much space you will have on the tables.

When measuring your space, take some visual references of the type of style and decoration you want, and measure items such as windowsills, pedestals, table lengths and widths. If you are hiring a function space such as a village hall, it may include furniture in the hire cost. If so, check it over, count the chairs and roughly lay out the room to see how many people can seat comfortably and where the food, bar and DJ will be positioned. Take pictures as you go so you can show the space to anyone else who needs to visualise it – it will also help to remind you later on. Try not to rush the measuring and visualising; it may seem tedious, but it is crucial to get it right. You might also want to make some simple sketches as you measure out the room, to log where everything will fit.

Once you have worked out how your spaces will work and the decorations they need, you can total up the quantities, and work out what to make and what to buy (see page 16). Remember that you will need to allow time to try out some of your ideas in the actual position to check for fit and visual impact. I did this with the church pompom flowers. I made a few examples in different colour sequences, then hung them in position in the church. I took some photographs, made sure I was happy, then made the rest.

(see page 16)

TIP:
FURNITURE FIT

Hiring space-efficient furniture can make a big difference. We hired folding chairs: not only were they small so that they took up minimal space in the hall, but they also folded up neatly and stacked away when they weren't needed in the evening. Tables also come in many sizes, large and small, so check what is available and double check that something of a different size wouldn't work better.

TIP:
CHANGING SPACES

If you need to rearrange furniture at different points in the day, plan the layout to make things as easy as possible. We had to dismantle some of the tables and chairs in the evening to make space for a dance floor. Note the tasks down and delegate jobs to your wedding party or staff.

Below: after measuring our venue, I sketched out some ideas for how to hang the bunting, inside and out, so that I could measure up these arrangements on a second visit.

Right: my initial ideas for how our room might work with different shaped tables, along with the final room plan.

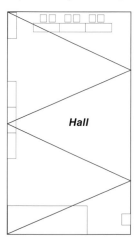

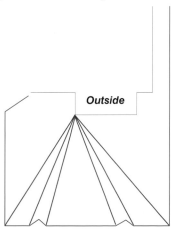

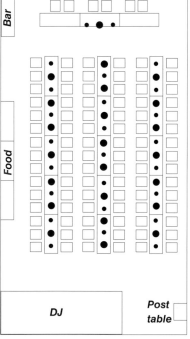

MAKE OR BUY?

It can be hard to decide what to make or buy if you are particularly crafty and love making things as much as I do. Consider the time it will take, the money it will cost, and the nature of the venue itself. If it is a blank canvas requiring a lot of decoration, such as a village hall, it will take a long time to make all that you need, so hiring, borrowing or buying some items might be your best option.

Create a master list

Make a list of all the things you need so that you can decide what to make and what to buy. Research each element of your wedding, decide what you want and work out what to source from suppliers and what to make yourself and with help from friends and family. I've included my rough list, right. This list is quite extensive and you may not need nearly as many elements. For example, you might not need favours or chair covers, your venue might provide signage and tablecloths, and you could leave the guests to bring their own confetti. There are many ways to keep your day simple and on budget, and I find it is easiest to consider every element first, and then eliminate the unnecessary items.

It is a good idea to keep your list up to date with weblinks, images and contact details so at any time you can pick it up and reference it. This will be particularly useful when it comes to arranging and checking up on the larger elements of the day. I suggest buying a wedding planner notebook. Mine became filled with all my supplier details, what had to be purchased, dates of suit fittings and dress fittings and also where I had bought craft supplies so I knew exactly where to go for repeat purchases. Choose one that is sturdy, as it will be carted about everywhere you go, and will quickly get filled up. Alternatively, use your smartphone or tablet to compile all the information digitally.

Items to consider...

- Save the date cards
- Invitations
- Orders of service
- Hair accessories for all the wedding party: fabric flowers, tiaras, combs, headbands
- Veil
- Buttonholes/boutonnieres
- Corsages
- Bouquets
- Flowers for the ceremony: church pew ends, windowsill arrangements, outdoor garlands, pedestals
- Confetti
- Confetti cones and display box
- Ring pillow
- Reception table flowers
- Vases for table flowers
- Table cloths
- Chairs and chair covers
- Room decoration: bunting, pompoms
- Wedding cake
- Wedding desserts
- Cake toppers
- Signage for the hall
- Place names
- Table plan
- Favours
- Children's party favour bags
- Paper decoupage top table decoration: MR and MRS
- Chalkboard timetable
- Clothing: dresses, suits, ties, waistcoats, shoes, bags
- Wedding rings

Pricing up your options

It is important to know how much things will cost to buy, hire or make, especially those items that you will need in large quantities and that may be time-consuming to make. If like me you want bunting for your reception venue, you must measure the venue and draw up a rough plan to work out the length you need. Then, compare the price of buying or hiring the quantity required, and the cost of buying all the fabrics, threads and ribbons to make it yourself. Look at online haberdashery and fabric shops for quotes as they are often much cheaper than high street stores; local markets may also be a good source of cheap fabric. Quantity is often what will help you decide if you have the time or budget to make something yourself.

In my case, I needed 300m (984ft) of bunting to decorate the reception venue inside and out. This was a lot to afford if buying or hiring, but also a lot in quantity to make. I bought the fabric from our local market and the rest of the supplies online and it cost only £100 (about $150). To hire it would have been closer to five times this price. It took a long time to make, but for me the results were worth it.

Delegating

Consider who might like to help you out and delegate a few tasks to crafty friends and family. Make a list of the items you are hoping to make and allocate each item with names of those people who could help you. When doing this, keep in mind the skills of each person you enlist and try not to overburden them with monotonous, repetitive tasks, as this may cause them to rush and create a dip in quality.

Sourcing second-hand items

On some social media sites, volunteers have created pages dedicated to selling unused or 'used just once' wedding paraphernalia. This can be a brilliant way to cut costs and you can often find items that are on trend, such as glass candy jars, scoops and bags to create your own traditional candy stall, or sets of items, such as matching vases for centrepieces. The sites are often named by county or area so search online to see whether there are any near you. Also, bear this option in mind as a way of making some of your money back after the wedding (see page 122).

Storing items

Consider how much storage space you have, as this will help to determine how far in advance you can make or buy things. If you plan to make an abundance of large items, and need to make them well in advance, you may need to call in favours from friends or family. My old bedroom at my parents' house was empty, so all of the church flowers were made months in advance and stored there in large bin bags and boxes, covering every surface I could make use of.

TIP:
SAFE STORE
Avoid storing your crafts in garages or roof spaces. The changes in humidity and temperature can degrade glues, papers and other materials, which could ruin your hard work. Always cover everything over, as sunlight is also very damaging and can bleach out the colours.

PLANNING YOUR TIME

Whether you are planning your wedding in eight or eighteen months, a clear time plan will help you keep on top of things. Some tasks, like dress alterations, take a set amount of time, and you will need to book elements such as your photographer and caterer well in advance, so it's important to have an idea of the overall time frame. Use this planner as a rough guide so that you can leave yourself plenty of time for your crafty jobs.

Before drawing up a production timetable, think about items that can be made or stored in advance, such as paper flowers, and non-food based favours. Home-dried petals for confetti may need to be scheduled in when the garden is flowering. A handmade veil may need to be made or mocked up ready for a dress fitting. Think each item through and, if you can, give it a rough date. Equally, don't get too stressed if it isn't on schedule – some things will take less time, and others more, so you may find that you catch up later, and if not, get people to help you or cancel something on your list and buy it instead. I just made as much as I could as quickly as I could, starting with the items I needed most of – for me it was flowers and bunting.

TIP:
GENTLE REMINDERS
Write in your diary the number of days remaining, or set a countdown on your phone, to help spur you on and keep you on target.

My basic time plan

12 MONTHS TO GO

- ✽ Work out your budget
- ✽ Pick a wedding date and book your venues
- ✽ Organise the wedding license and book the registrar, if necessary
- ✽ Choose your theme and plan what you will need to buy or make
- ✽ Start planning your guestlist
- ✽ Ask your bridesmaids and groomsmen to be part of the wedding party
- ✽ **MAKE YOUR SAVE THE DATES**

8–10 MONTHS TO GO

- ✽ Order your dress
- ✽ Book the photographer, videographer, caterer, florist and any entertainment such as band or DJ
- ✽ Order the cake, if you are not making one
- ✽ Block-book hotel rooms for out-of-town guests
- ✽ Consider setting up a wedding website
- ✽ Send out your save the dates
- ✽ **MAKE YOUR INVITATIONS**

With 8 MONTHS to go, I started making all the flowers and pompoms for the church and reception: I spent most spare evenings and weekends making flowers...

With about 7 MONTHS to go, I made my candle wedding favours with my mother-in-law, and got the bunting underway...

6 MONTHS TO GO

- ✽ Book your transport
- ✽ Choose the bridesmaids' dresses
- ✽ Choose the men's outfits and accessories
- ✽ Choose your shoes and accessories
- ✽ **MAKE YOUR TABLE DECORATIONS**
- ✽ Choose your readings
- ✽ Send out your invitations
- ✽ Book your honeymoon
- ✽ Register your gift list

With about 6 MONTHS to go, I mocked up my first flower table decoration, to give myself an idea of how many more I needed to make....

With about **5 MONTHS** to go I made our buttonholes/boutonnieres and stored them in biscuit tins! And I completed all the bouquets...

With about **4 MONTHS** to go, I checked the colour of the buttonholes/boutonnieres against the suits and ties. I also trialled the first set of pew ends in the church, before making the rest...

3 MONTHS TO GO

- ❀ Purchase the wedding rings
- ❀ Order your favours if you are not making them
- ❀ Book your first night hotel
- ❀ Finalise your guestlist
- ❀ Devise a seating plan
- ❀ Book hair and make-up consultations

With **3 MONTHS** to go, I completed my reception flowers and made the vases to display them in.

2 MONTHS TO GO

- ❀ Finalise the menu
- ❀ Decide on the music for the ceremony and for the reception
- ❀ **MAKE OR BUY THANK YOU GIFTS FOR THE WEDDING PARTY**
- ❀ Attend the final dress fitting with accessories

With **2 MONTHS** to go, I made my veil and hair piece, ready for my final dress fitting. I also made my ring pillow, the decoupage Mr and Mrs for the top table, my confetti cones and confetti box.

With about **6 WEEKS** to go, I did a trial run of my cakes, and ordered my baking equipment.

4 WEEKS TO GO

- ❀ Give your venue copies of supplier contracts
- ❀ **MAKE YOUR PLACE CARDS**
- ❀ Discuss duties with the best man, ushers and bridesmaids
- ❀ Have your hen do and stag do
- ❀ Write your vows

With about **4 WEEKS** to go, I completed my chalkboard timetable.

THE LAST FEW WEEKS

- ❀ Discuss the photographs you want your photographer to capture
- ❀ Confirm everything: your honeymoon, venue, ceremony and all your suppliers
- ❀ **MAKE YOUR CAKE**
- ❀ Have the cake delivered, if you are not making one
- ❀ With 1–3 days remaining, have a wedding rehearsal at the venue

I would suggest trying to get most tasks – other than the cake – completed by the last two weeks, as this is the time when final details will need to be confirmed with all your suppliers. You will need time to collect outfits, plan your set-up and take care of any last-minute changes. I took the week off work before our wedding: I baked, iced and stacked the cakes, and made all the sugar flower decorations. With a couple of days to go, I filled the candy jars, and started to box things up ready for set-up day. I also wrote up a groom's timetable and a bride's timetable.

THE DAY BEFORE
- ❀ Decorate the venue and the tables

THE MARRIAGE OF

MARRIANNE MERCER

and

DAVID MIALL

ST MARY'S CHURCH
LEIGH

3PM, FRIDAY 2ND AUGUST
2013

MARRIANNE MERCER

and

DAVID MIALL

JOYFULLY INVITE YOU TO THEIR

WEDDING

CELEBRATION

SAVE the DATE

02.08.2013

MARRIANNE & DAVID

ARE GETTING

MARRIED!

INVITATION TO FOLLOW

THE STATIONERY

Whether you decide to make your own, use a bought set, or do away with paper altogether and organise your whole day online, the first item to consider must be your save the dates. So from your draft headcount, make a more final list with the contact details of all your guests. If you can, it's a good idea to tie all your items of stationery together, so try to think about an overall style, colour or theme right at the start.

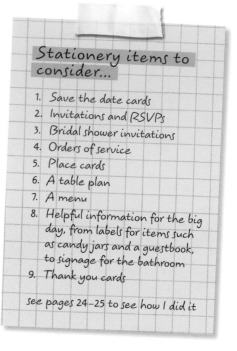

WHY MAKE YOUR OWN STATIONERY?

Quite simply, if you make your own stationery it will be unique, you can easily keep it on a budget, and you will have complete control over adjusting any last-minute changes. Shop-bought stationery tends to be very 'safe' in its design, and custom-designed stationery comes at a price. As a DIY bride I didn't want either of these options. I saw this as the ideal opportunity to save huge amounts of money, to set our style and to give our guests a little hint of how colourful, unique and hand-crafted our day was going to be.

Make a plan

Start by making a list of all the stationery you will need. Also think about how many of each item you need to make. If you have 100 guests, the chances are you'll need to make 100 place cards and orders of service, but only around fifty to sixty save the dates and invitations, as most guests are coupled or come with children. Your guest list will be useful, but you need to work out a set number of invitations to send out and then add a few spares. The spares are useful if any invitations get lost in the post or if guests misplace them; additionally, if anyone declines, you will easily be able to invite other guests to take their place. Having a total will help you to decide if a computer-generated creation is a good alternative to hand-making a design with lots of embellishments. Handmade stationery can take a long time, so bear that in mind.

Do your research

Research different wedding stationery styles and collect examples of what you like – you can then incorporate different ideas and pull them together into your own design. To create a unified theme it is a good idea to give each item of stationery similar styling by using matching elements such as colours, fonts and motifs across all of them. You don't have to design all the stationery in one go, but it is sensible to have a few ideas or templates drawn up so that when you do get round to making items, it will be a quicker process.

Choose a motif

If, like me, you tend to get overwhelmed with lots of initial ideas, you might want to simplify your design by choosing a motif. As ours was a village fête wedding, I wanted an abundance of flowers and colour, so I used these in my stationery designs. Think about what inspires you and come up with a similar motif or recurring shape, colour, pattern or photograph that runs throughout.

Stationery items to consider...

1. Save the date cards
2. Invitations and RSVPs
3. Bridal shower invitations
4. Orders of service
5. Place cards
6. A table plan
7. A menu
8. Helpful information for the big day, from labels for items such as candy jars and a guestbook, to signage for the bathroom
9. Thank you cards

see pages 24–25 to see how I did it

TIP:
BE PAPER SAVVY
To save money, always be economical with paper. If you decide to cut out little motifs to stick on each invitation, line them up and cut out as many as possible from one sheet of paper.

Online design

If you struggle with design but stationery is something you want to create for yourself, there are websites that create custom designs for you. You can choose a size and then upload an image and add your text. The site will show you some pre-designed formats and allow you to create a design more unique than a shop-bought item; however, this can be quite a pricey option.

Things to think about…

1. Number of guests?
Don't overburden yourself with an elaborate handmade design if you have lots to make. You may well get bored and run out of time before the rest of the process has even started! Equally, think about the cost of all those embellishments.

2. What exactly do you need?
Make a list of the materials and equipment you will need. You may want to simplify your design if it's looking too costly. Also, think about other pieces of stationery that will have a similar look. If you buy materials all together you are likely to save money, even if it is just the delivery cost.

3. What is the cost?
Do your research and buy the materials where you find them at the best price – don't just rush out and buy them in the nearest store.

4. When is it needed by?
Don't sit on the save the dates or invitations for too long or you won't have any guests at your wedding! Remember, you need the RSVPs in plenty of time to inform caterers of final numbers and to confirm table plan arrangements.

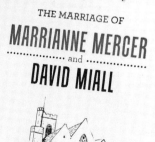

THE MARRIAGE OF

MARRIANNE MERCER
and

DAVID MIALL

ST MARY'S CHURCH,
LEIGH

3PM, FRIDAY 2ND AUGUST
2013

KEY STATIONERY ITEMS

Save the dates

These go out before the formal invitation and are simply an announcement of who is getting married and when – the venue and timings are given later on the full invitation. You may want to title it 'save the date' so that people understand that it is not the formal invitation; I also included the text 'invitation to follow', just to be sure. Send your save the dates out as soon as you have a date confirmed, so that your guests can keep it free. You could skip this step altogether and just send invitations, but if your wedding is a little way off and you want to guarantee attendance, it's a good idea as it gives people notice not to book in other events.

I designed my save the dates as postcards. They were double-sided and postcard-sized (14 x 10cm / 5½ x 4in) to save on material costs – this also meant that we didn't need envelopes, as I wrote the guests' addresses on the back. If you design your save the dates yourself, set the tone for your other wedding stationery and perhaps use design elements, colours and images that you plan on using elsewhere. I used fabrics as backgrounds that were later seen in the bunting, table runners and candle favour lids.

Invitations

The design of your invitation can be as ornate or as simple as you like, but ultimately the information it needs to contain is quite straightforward. It should detail whose wedding it is and who is inviting them – traditionally invitations are sent on behalf of the bride and groom by the bride's parents, though this is not always the case – the specific names of those invited, the date, place and time of the ceremony, as well as the details of where and what time the reception will be. You will need to create separate versions for guests who will be invited to the whole event, and those who are invited to the evening reception only. On the back of our invitations I also included the RSVP date and our gift list information. I sent the invitations out as soon as we had confirmed the timings of our wedding, giving our guests about three months to respond.

I really went to town with the design of our invitation; I kept the rest of the pages – the RSVP card and further information – much simpler, but followed the same design theme. If you are not including a dedicated RSVP card, you will need to detail a responding postal or email address, and a date to respond by.

RSVPs

You don't have to send out an RSVP card with your invitation – many people simply rely on their guests to send a card, email or message back, or create a wedding website, so that they can manage everything online. I decided I would send out cards because I felt it made the process easier for my guests, and might make for a swifter return time – I didn't want to waste precious crafting time chasing up guests who hadn't responded.

You need to include the name of the bride and groom, the wedding date and the date you need the RSVPs back by – I wanted a reply two months before our wedding date to give me time to finalise the catering numbers and table plans.

I made the RSVPs in the same postcard format as our save the date cards. I reiterated all the key details on the front, and on the back I created a little fill-in form so that guests could state whether they were accepting or declining the invitation, list their names, and fill in the number of adults and the number of children. I also asked for the children's ages so that I could put a little party bag together for each child to keep them entertained during the speeches. I added our home address and an email address, for people who preferred to respond in their own way, remembering to allow space for stamps.

Useful information

Our invitation held a huge amount of information about our day and the local area so that our guests had an easy time finding us. As the wedding was in a relatively rural location, we didn't want our guests getting lost or causing any friction with the local villagers by parking anywhere that they shouldn't. We wrote out directions to the village from major roads in the area and we included a detailed map of the village showing the venues and the useful landmarks, road names and specified parking areas. We collected information about the local train times and fares from the nearest town, as well as a list of taxi cab firms with contact details and prices. We contacted a few local hotels and gave their addresses, contact numbers, room prices and a list of pros and cons to help people decide which accommodation was best for them.

I created a whole pamphlet of information that was approximately A5 (5¾ x 8⅓in) in size. To be economical when printing I chose A3 (11¾ x 16½in) sized card, which was the largest the printer could take. I then copied and pasted several of the same A5 (5¾ x 8⅓in) designs onto an A3 (11¾ x 16½in) size document and printed it double-sided. I then cut out each piece of information to become A5 (5¾ x 8⅓in) double-sided cards. I joined them in the corner with card makers' split pins.

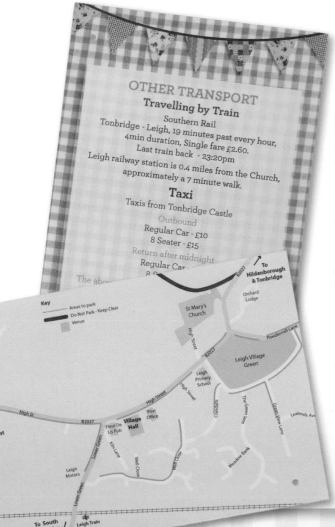

Order of service

The order of service is usually completed last, and within only a couple of weeks of the big day. Ours outlined whose marriage it was, dates, times and the location on the front cover, followed by a single folded A4 (8^1/$_3$ x 11^2/$_3$in) sheet, printed on both sides. The inner pages outlined the entire ceremony, who was doing readings and all the words to the songs. The back cover had a list of thank yous and onward instructions for the reception.

Orders of service do not need envelopes, so to make it easy, we printed the covers two per A3 (11¾ x 16½in) piece of card, the same as all the other stationery. The inside section was printed double-sided onto a standard A4 (8^1/$_3$ x 11^2/$_3$in) sheet of paper. This was then folded in half and stuck into the centre fold of the cover using a strip of double-sided tape. As you can see, I followed some of the styling ideas that were used for the other stationery, using the gingham background, and little embellishments such as bunting and flowers.

THE MARRIAGE OF

MARRIANNE MERCER

and

DAVID MIALL

ST MARY'S CHURCH, LEIGH

3PM, FRIDAY 2ND AUGUST 2013

He gave us eyes to see them,
And lips that we might tell,
How great is God Almighty,
Who has made all things well.
All things bright...

READING BY DONNA CUTHBERTSON
John 2: Verses 1-11

ADDRESS

MARRIAGE VOWS & THE EXCHANGE OF RINGS

HYMN - GUIDE ME O THOU GREAT REDEEMER

Guide me, O thou great redeemer,
Pilgrim through this barren land;
I am weak, but thou art mighty,
Hold me with thy powerful hand;
Bread of heaven, bread of heaven
Feed me till I want no more;
Feed me till I want no more.

Open now the crystal fountain
Whence the healing stream doth flow;
Let the fire and cloudy pillar
Lead me all my journey through:
Strong deliverer, strong deliverer;
Be thou still my strength and shield;
Be thou still my strength and shield.

When I tread the verge of Jordan,
Bid my anxious fears subside;
Death of death, and hell's destruction
Land me safe on Canaan's side:
Songs of praises, songs of praises,
I will ever give to thee;
I will ever give to thee.

PRAYERS
Followed by

THE LORD'S PRAYER

Our Father in heaven,
hallowed be your name,
your kingdom come,
your will be done,
on earth as in heaven.
Give us today our daily bread.
Forgive us our sins
as we forgive those who sin against us.
Lead us not into temptation
but deliver us from evil.
For the kingdom, the power,
and the glory are yours
now and forever.
Amen.

HYMN - ONE MORE STEP ALONG THE WORLD I GO

One more step along the world I go,
one more step along the world I go;
from the old things to the new
keep me travelling along with you:
*Refrain: And it's from the old I travel to the new;
keep me travelling along with you.*

Round the corner of the world I turn,
more and more about the world I learn;
all the new things that I see
you'll be looking at along with me: *Refrain*

Continued overleaf...

Thank you cards

I didn't think about these properly until after our wedding, as they just weren't a priority. However, I knew that I wanted them to fit in the same size envelopes that the invitations went out in, so that I could purchase a bulk quantity of them. I had in mind that I was going to keep it simple and use one of our professional pictures on the front. See page 120.

CHOOSING YOUR MATERIALS

Before you rush out and buy anything, have a think about how you want your stationery to look and feel. Visit wedding fairs, browse bridal magazines and search online to get ideas and start to work out what you want.

Paper and card

How sturdy do you want your stationery to feel; and if you are creating it on a computer, how will it be printed? If you print it at home, make sure you check your printer capabilities. Most printers are set up to print on standard 80gsm (0.2lb) everyday paper but may have settings in the print dialogue that allow for heavier weights, so check before buying your card. Equally, copy shop printers will have limitations. Think about the texture of your paper or card. Anything that has large ridges or a bumpy texture may not print very well. Sometimes the simplest papers are best. See the box, right, for advice on the pros and cons of different weights.

Envelopes

I would advise that you choose your invitation size based on the envelopes available. Otherwise you could create an invitation that is loose inside its envelope, which might get bent and crumpled in the post. If you want to make your own envelopes, you can find instructions online. I decided against making my own. After all, the envelope doesn't need to be more than a protective cover for a beautiful invitation, and will probably end up thrown away, so you may not want to get too precious about them. I chose my cardstock based on the size of invitation I was going to make, so that I could be economical and create minimal waste. I wanted to make it an approximate A5 (5¾ x 8⅓in) size. The nearest envelope size was C6 (4½ x 6½in), which is slightly smaller, but meant that there was minimal wastage when printing onto A3 (11¾ x 16½in) card and cutting out.

Card weights

Light-weight card weighs up to 170gsm (0.4lb). This would be ideal if you decide to make a card that is traditional in structure and folds in half. It will allow you to give it a crisp clean fold. When it is folded it will still feel and look sturdy.

Mid-weight card weighs between about 170gsm (0.4lb) and 220gsm (0.5lb). It might be best to print information on it and then layer it onto a decorative base of thicker card.

Heavy-weight card weighs from around 220gsm (0.5lb) to 285gsm (0.6lb) and this is now almost too thick to bend neatly. This is ideal for making single piece flat invitations, like ours. The card is thick enough to hold itself without being folded, so would make a good postcard, and feels good quality on its own. Just be sure the printer you use can take the weight. I used 225gsm (0.5lb).

Decorative papers

You can print straight onto light-weight decorative papers and they provide an interesting change to plain white; choose subtle tones so that your words stand out well. If you want to incorporate more elaborate and highly patterned papers, you could cut motifs out of them and glue them onto a simple design to add a bit of interest. Heavier-weight decorative papers are ideal as you can mount other pieces of paper onto them, for a premium feel. There are lots on the market, from handmade card made from recycled paper and containing dried leaves or flowers, to quality high-end textured paper with scalloped edges and pre-fold marks.

Where to buy

Most local craft stores sell a range of papers and cards. It's a good idea to go and look at them, feel them and get an idea of how you might use them in your design. You could always buy one or two examples and try them out. It's a question of trial and error, weighing up the time they take to make with the finished look. Once you've worked out what you want, I would suggest looking online to compare the price of buying the rest of your materials, to make sure you're getting the best value for money.

Recycling and upcycling

These are such fantastic cost-cutting techniques – you will feel like you've created something really special for nothing. Here are a few ideas to get you started: use **old newspapers** as your decorative paper motif or as a backing paper to a plain printed invitation. Mount your information onto old **card or paper magazine samples**. If you have any spare **textiles** lying around, such as scraps of felt or an old nightshirt, cut them up and use them as decorative embellishments or cut them into **ribbons**. Find your grandmother's button tin and stick one or two **buttons** onto the invitation to add a bit of interest. You could use **garden string** to tie the invitation pieces together. Look around at home in your stationery drawer – you may be surprised what you find and how creative you can be with it.

TIP:
WEIGH IT UP

Remember when choosing the weight of paper and all the extra embellishments that the heavier and larger the invitation, the more it will cost to post. Remind yourself of local postage fees before you start.

TIP:
MIX IT UP

Bear in mind when sourcing materials that each invitation can be slightly or even totally different, so don't worry if you feel you can't find enough of any one material to complete 50 invitations. The guest will never know what everyone else received.

CREATING A COMPUTER DESIGN

As a graphic designer, I have access to professional desktop publishing software, which made the design and creation of our stationery very easy. My boss was kind enough to let me to use the software in my personal time to create our pieces and then print them at work. I bought my own paper and envelopes and paid for the colour printing, and this made it a much cheaper option than taking the designs to a copy shop. Ask friends, family and colleagues if they might be able to help in this way. I used software called Adobe Indesign; the next best thing on most home computers would be Microsoft Word. Here are three simple routes to take if you want to create computer-generated stationery.

TIP:
FANCY FONTWORK

For those of you who are confident with computers, try viewing and downloading some new fonts, as these will give your designs a real lift and a sense of style. Search online for 'free font downloads' – there are lots to choose from.

Design option one

Type the text, add some images or motifs and create a simple design; print it on textured, coloured or patterned paper or card. The look and feel of the design can be fun or elegant depending on the paper you have chosen. Here I have added a fun element to the design with the choice of pink stripy paper, but you could change this to give a completely different appearance. This is a great way to save printing costs too, as you can keep your designs completely black and let the paper choice be the splash of colour. You can buy pre-folded cards that can be put through a home printer, which is a great way to save time. Always test a few first to check that you are happy with them, and that the printer prints with the correct margins. You don't want to buy sixty pre-folded cards and then discover your printer won't print on them!

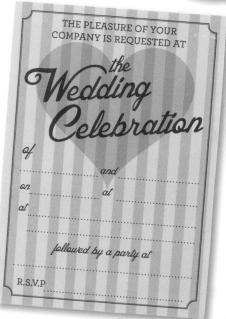

This is the simplest invitation you can achieve, and it can be made far in advance as the details are written on by hand when you are ready.

This design is stylish and fun. I have created a simple double-sided design, which has a simple, striking design on the front, with all the essential details on the back.

This design requires only a photocopier and some patterned paper, making it a good option if you don't have regular access to a computer. A fun black and white design with some downloaded fonts sets the theme.

Design option two

This involves creating the same design as in option one – perhaps with some colour added – but printing it onto a single layer of simple paper and then layering it onto a piece of decorative card that is cut slightly larger. Stick the print-out onto the card so that it acts like a frame around the information. This works really well when the card is cut to A5 (5¾ x 8⅓in) in size and your print-out is 2cm (¾in) smaller both vertically and horizontally to give a 1cm (½in) frame all round. You can be quite creative here and use a beautiful card stock and even print the text onto a coloured paper. You can then embellish the two layers with pieces of ribbon or diamantés to help soften the hard lines of the layering. You could also make a hole in the top left corner and tie a ribbon through it to attach an RSVP card.

This design is made stylish with the use of simple illustrations along with the ribbon and lace embellishments. A small diamanté finishes off the overall look by adding a little sparkle.

If you would like to use pre-folded cards but your printer won't print on them, why not add printed layers and embellish them by hand instead? Here I have used a pearlised card and attached a simple design with double-sided tape. The design is finished off with ribbon and sticky hearts (above).

The inside (left) is a piece of paper cut 5mm (¼in) smaller on all sides, with the details printed on it.

Design option three

If you can't get the desired look on screen, or perhaps lack the necessary computer skills, this could be the option for you. Print out all the typed information, leaving plenty of space around each element. Cut out all the individual lines or groups of text and arrange them on a piece of paper the correct size. You can then photocopy this layout yourself if you have access to a good-quality copy machine, or you could take it to a copy shop to print on a card or paper of your choice. You can still be creative with this and play around with the type size, colour, weight or font style.

You can still make your photocopied design into a handmade invitation. Here the photocopied arrangement has been stuck onto a decorative paper, along with some papercraft decorative corners. I framed one side with a piece of natural ribbon and lace, followed by some sticky flowers. Colour and texture like this can make a design far more interesting and eye-catching.

Marrianne Mercer
AND David Miall
JOYFULLY INVITE YOU TO THEIR
WEDDING CELEBRATION
FRIDAY 2ND AUGUST 2013
AT 3PM IN THE AFTERNOON
ST MARY'S CHURCH,
LEIGH, TONBRIDGE KENT TN11 8OJ
FOLLOWED BY A KNEES UP AT
LEIGH VILLAGE HALL

Adding embellishments

With each of these options you can still add embellishments afterwards. These can help to lift the design, make it more interesting and give a further hint towards the theme of the wedding. Look online or in your local craft store at the card-making embellishments. You will find buttons, ribbons, motifs, rubber stamps, flowers and diamantés – all sorts to give your designs a twist.

Wedding Invitation

Wedding Invitation

MR & MRS JOHN MERCER
REQUEST THE PLEASURE OF YOUR COMPANY AT
THE MARRIAGE OF THEIR DAUGHTER
Marrianne Linda Mercer
TO
David John James Miall
FRIDAY SECOND AUGUST TWO THOUSAND & THIRTEEN
AT THREE O'CLOCK IN THE AFTERNOON
ST MARY'S CHURCH,
LEIGH, TONBRIDGE KENT TN11 8QJ
RECEPTION IMMEDIATELY FOLLOWING
AT LEIGH VILLAGE HALL

CREATING A HANDMADE DESIGN

This design incorporates a mix of computer design and hands-on crafty embellishment. You could easily adapt it to your own colour scheme and theme by changing the colours, textures and patterns of each layer. You could also remove the computer-designed layer and instead create a wonderful handwritten or stencilled text layer.

Get your fiancé, friends and family to help with the creation of these, and remember it is cheaper to buy larger pieces of card and paper and cut them to size than it is to buy ready-cut pieces. Think about using up spare paper, gift wrap or even wallpaper samples to make each invitation slightly different. The white scalloped edge layer on this design was actually created from a roll of gift wrap that I laid out to flatten for a day and then cut to size.

What you need per card

- ⊕ A5 (5¾ x 8⅓in) sheet of pearlescent turquoise card
- ⊕ 137 x 198mm (5¼ x 7¾in) piece of patterned paper
- ⊕ A5 (5¾ x 8⅓in) sheet of white textured paper
- ⊕ Scalloped template, see page 124
- ⊕ Printed design on light blue paper, cut to 100 x 164mm (4 x 6½in)
- ⊕ 20cm (8in) length of 3cm (1¼in) wide turquoise ribbon
- ⊕ 45cm (17½in) length of 3cm (1¼in) wide cream lace
- ⊕ A button of your choice
- ⊕ Twenty-four 3mm (⅛in) adhesive stones
- ⊕ Spray mount or double-sided tape
- ⊕ Hot glue gun

Instructions

1 Cut the card and paper layers to size. Photocopy or trace off the scalloped template from page 124 and cut it out. Draw around this template onto the back of your A5 (5¾ x 8⅓in) piece of white textured paper, so that any pencil marks will be hidden. Cut the scalloped edge.

2 Secure your patterned paper centrally on top of your turquoise pearlescent card with either spray mount or double-sided tape; spray mount is my preferred option as you can easily adjust the positioning. Spray on top of a piece of scrap paper to protect your work surface.

3 Secure your textured, scalloped paper on top of the first two layers with spray mount or double-sided tape.

TIP: SPACED OUT

When creating your text layer, remember to leave a large enough gap in the information for your ribbon to run through. See the finished card, right. Print out your design and experiment with different widths of ribbon before you commit to printing all the invitations.

You are invited to

the Wedding of

MARRIANNE MERCER
&
DAVID MIALL

ON FRIDAY 2ND AUGUST 2013 AT 3PM
ST MARY'S CHURCH, LEIGH, TONBRIDGE KENT TN11 8QJ
RECEPTION IMMEDIATELY FOLLOWING
AT LEIGH VILLAGE HALL
R.S.V.P XXXXXX

TIP:
GATHERING SPEED
If you are making lots of this invitation, get a production line of each stage going, as you will get quicker each time you repeat it.

4 Secure your piece of text on top with spray mount or double-sided tape. Double check that your ribbon fits neatly between your areas of text, with enough length to fold the ends over onto the back. Apply double-sided tape to the top and bottom edges of your ribbon, then stick it in place; secure the ribbon ends neatly on the back.

5 Apply a piece of double-sided tape across the centre of your ribbon. Starting from the right-hand side, leave a small amount of lace to tuck round to the back of the card, then stick the lace down until you come to the centre point. Fold the lace back on itself by about 6cm (2¼in) and then back again to form a loop.

6 With this lace loop still positioned on the right, create another lace loop of the same size and continue to stick down the rest of the lace, as shown. Secure each end of the lace to the back of the card, as you did for the ribbon.

7 Rearrange the lace so that it lies centrally, and looks like a very neat, flat bow shape. Using your hot glue gun, stick your button of choice in the middle of your bow using a pea-sized amount of glue. If your button has a shank, cut this off with wire cutters or strong scissors beforehand.

8 Finish off your design by sticking an adhesive diamanté onto each of the scalloped shapes.

THE WEDDING PARTY

Organising people is by far the hardest challenge of any handmade wedding. Everybody has an opinion, they all feel they should share it with you, and their first question is usually 'what am I wearing?' As the bride and groom, it's your day to shine, and you need those around you to help that happen.

My advice to you is to stick to your guns and ask people to go with the flow. If you have a certain 'look' to accomplish, go for it, and hope that people are willing to help you achieve it. If making the outfits is a bit beyond you and your helpers' skills, think about all the accessories you could make instead that will be unique and on budget.

Buttonholes/boutonnieres can be expensive, mainly because traditionally they are made from fresh flowers, which means the florist has to allocate time solely to your flowers a few hours before the wedding. Instead, why not make your own from paper or fabric? They could be something more personal to you both than a flower, or could be something jewelled, made of buttons, feathers or dried leaves. Being a DIY bride means you can think outside the box and make things that are unique and exceptional – your guests might even be able to keep them long after the wedding as keepsakes.

WHERE TO START?

Clothing and accessorising your bridal party can be a very expensive headache. What type of dress do you want? Do you want a veil? What style of suit does your groom want? Does he want a waistcoat? What bridesmaid dresses do you choose? In what colour? With flat shoes or high sandals? Buttonholes/boutonnieres, cravats and pocket squares? There are so many different options and colour ways to consider.

Keeping your theme and colour palette in mind, research real weddings and ideas online and see what inspires you. Think about choosing a colour for the outfits that complements all the other decorations, but also look at how you can tie the ladies and gentlemen of the wedding party together visually. If the bridesmaids have blue dresses, perhaps the groomsmen could have blue ties and handkerchiefs? If you are choosing dresses from a particular era – for example, mine were 1950s inspired – do you want the suits to also reflect some of this vintage styling?

Rent, buy or make?

Hiring the groomsmen's suits is an affordable option, although there are plenty of companies that make bespoke suits, if your groom wants a more personalised option. Making the dresses for the ladies is the biggest potential money saver, although it is a big undertaking and would require a lot of patience and skill. If making the dresses is out of the question, there are plenty of other ways in which you can keep the costs down. Many high street stores now have dedicated wedding departments, with good ranges at reasonable prices. Go and splash out on those beautiful dresses, but save money on the accessories.

Things to think about…

1. What items do you need?
Think carefully about what can be made, and what you want to buy. If you decide to make paper or fabric corsages, buttonholes/boutonnieres and bouquets, total up how many of each you need. Don't forget flower girls or page boys, who may need something too. Hair accessories can be easy to make – even a veil is super easy if you keep it simple. Will you need any other accessories for you or your bridesmaids? Little headbands with flowers attached for flower girls work well to unite them with the rest of the group. Will you need any jewellery?

2. When are the items needed by?
Ideally make these items as soon as you can. They can be quite delicate but as long as you have somewhere to store them, it will be another job done. If you decide to make your own hair piece and veil, make sure it is made in time for one of your dress fittings. It is a good idea to try everything on together to check the colour and whether you like it. I took a few fabric swatches to my first dress fitting and then the finished item to the final fitting.

3. How much can you afford to spend?
If your budget is relatively small then get crafting. If this is an area where you want to be more frivolous – perhaps selecting real flowers or designer shoes, then save your craftiness for other areas.

The bridal party

The best option for us was to rent the groomsmen's suits and top pocket handkerchiefs and buy the bridesmaids' dresses. I made almost everything else, including the paper flowers for the bouquets, buttonholes/boutonnieres and corsages. I also made the fabric flower hair accessories for myself and the bridesmaids; I made the hair flowers for the bridesmaids in the same colour as the groomsmen's handkerchiefs and ties, which helped tie everyone together.

As for every bride, I imagine, my dress was very important to me. This was one of the few things that didn't come out of our budget as my parents insisted that it was their contribution to our day. It wasn't cheap and therefore, making budget-friendly accessories was very high up on my agenda to keep a lid on the expenses.

TIP:
SHOE SAVINGS
Shoes can also be an expense. But if you and your bridesmaids are wearing long gowns, who's going to see your shoes anyway? If you want to bring the price down, buy last season's trend or visit a high street store for shoes that you might all wear again.

TIP:
TYING EVERYONE TOGETHER
We had a best woman, rather than a best man. We made sure she still looked like part of the party by putting her in a dress that matched the colour of the groomsmen's ties and handkerchiefs and teamed it with a grey belt to match the men's grey suits.

FLORAL ACCESSORIES

Buttonholes/boutonnieres and corsages are traditionally worn by people with an important role on the wedding day; sometimes they are given to people as a symbol of thanks for their help and support during the wedding planning. They are generally made from the same variety of flower as the bride's bouquet, which is the ideal way to unify the wedding party. Some couples like to give one to all their guests, but this could create a lot of work for a DIY bride. During my research, I found that carnations and roses were the most popular flowers. However, there's nothing to stop you choosing a quirky non-floral option such as buttons, knotted string or brooches.

Who has which accessory?

Corsages

These are worn by the women in the party, usually the mothers of the bride and groom; I also made one for our best woman. Often they are worn pinned to the left breast – but they can also be worn on the wrist, in the hair, or just about anywhere. They are traditionally larger than a buttonhole/boutonniere, consisting of two or three flowers with foliage – I made mine with two paper gerberas: one pink, one orange. You might want to consider giving grandmothers and sisters a corsage to wear. If you want to be really organised you could find out the colour of their outfits in advance and match a lovely bloom to it.

Buttonholes/boutonnieres

These are traditionally worn by the groom, best man, ushers and the father of the bride. For everyone but the groom, they usually consist of just one flower worn on the left lapel of the suit jacket; I used one pink paper gerbera for each buttonhole/boutonniere. The groom's can be slightly larger than the others. I made Dave's with two paper flowers rather than one and used white gerberas to better complement my dress. Other important people such as grandparents, uncles and close family friends could be included on your list for buttonholes/boutonnieres, if you'd like them to be identified as part of the wedding party.

Flower girl's hair accessory

If you have flower girls in your wedding party, you might want to give them a small bouquet to hold or perhaps a small corsage or a floral hair accessory to wear. Consider the age of the girls: if they are too young, a bouquet may quickly be discarded. In some cases, a bracelet with a flower attached or a headband with a little matching flower on it would be best. You could even add an element of fun for the young ones and make a little wand with flowers or feathers on the end. Just be extremely careful not to give items with small, swallowable parts to very young children.

Bouquets

The bride has the largest bouquet and the bridesmaids often have smaller versions, or something slightly different in shape or colour. A large single flower, such as a peony, lily or gerbera carried by the bridesmaids can make a really beautiful change to the traditional type of bouquet, and would require relatively little cost and effort to make or buy.

Using real flowers

If you want to make your own accessories using real flowers, there are a few things to consider when choosing your design and flower variety, and you should always ask a florist for advice.

Will the flowers last all day?
If there's a chance they could wilt, you may need to come up with a solution to keep them hydrated. Investigate different flower types, as some are hardier than others.

Do any of the wedding party suffer from hayfever?
If they do, consider removing the pollen before assembling the accessory, or choose a flower that isn't too scented. Choose something leafy rather than floral.

How will they stay secured?
If you or any guests are wearing flowers in your hair, how will they be attached so that they stay there all day? Also, consider removing thorns or other uncomfortable parts.

Will the flowers damage your clothes?
Some flowers have heavy pollen that can fall onto your hair, skin or clothing and can permanently stain fabrics. Lily pollen in particular is notorious for this. If you know you want lilies, consider cutting the stamens out before wearing them – you won't want bright orange stains on your perfect white dress!

MAKING PAPER FLOWERS

Crepe paper flowers were the most important crafty item I wanted to make. This was what I started with as I knew it would take me the longest. I began with the reception table arrangements and soon realised that I could make the buttonholes/boutonnieres and bouquets in the same way.

Choose your favourite flowers

Gerberas are my favourite flowers and I learned that they are also the fastest to make, so when it came to making all the blooms for the bridal party accessories, they were the obvious choice (see pages 42–45). Gerberas became the focal flower of the wedding, and I made them in a variety of colours: pale pink, red, orange, yellow, white and dark pink. There are any number of different paper flower instructions available online – just do a quick search. Print pictures of what you like and see if you can recreate them for yourself. On pages 86–95, I've included the instructions for several paper flowers, made in lots of different materials, to inspire you and get you thinking.

Experiment

By the time I came to make the paper flowers for my bouquets, I had already made the gerberas for my centrepieces, so I had some examples to experiment with. I arranged several of them into bunches, to assess what I wanted. I tried various combinations of size and shape and added in little strips of green to complement the colours of the flowers. Doing this enabled me to make a rough total of how many gerberas I needed. I would strongly advise that you try making a few different types of flower,

and experiment with different arrangements, to find out what you like, but also to see how long it takes you to make them; bear in mind that with practice you should become faster over time.

I also tried different ways of making a buttonhole/boutonniere, asking myself questions such as: how large should it be? Does it need any foliage? Should I use one flower? Or two flowers? What type of ribbon should I tie it with? It's a great idea at this stage to experiment with materials, colours and ideas. Ask your fiancé to put on a suit jacket and pin one or two flowers against him to see what they look like and whether you both like the shape, size and colour.

Once I had worked out how many stems I needed for the accessories, I had to work out how many of each colour I needed. I made sure the corsages all had the same colour flowers, as did the flower girls' headbands and the men's buttonholes/boutonnieres. The bouquets were a mix of all the colours. I totalled up seventy-six flowers: twelve white, eighteen dark pink, ten light pink, thirteen yellow, thirteen orange and ten red. I tried to be economical with the materials: the bouquet flowers needed long wire stems, but the flowers for the rest of the accessories only needed short stems, so for these I was able to make two flowers with one wire.

Colour matching

Have your buttonholes/boutonnieres made in time to take to suit fittings, as you will get to see exactly what you'll have on the day. It will give you a bit of time to make any adjustments before the wedding if necessary, and if you take photographs, you'll also be able to reference and match any colours with the other members of the party. I took a fabric swatch of the bridesmaids' and best woman's outfits to the suit fitting, along with the groom's buttonhole/boutonniere. This enabled me to match the dress colour as closely as I could with the groomsmen's rented pocket squares and ties.

Storage

When storing your bouquets, remember that they will need plenty of space and should be kept in a dark, dry, dust-free place, to prevent the paper spoiling. I stored my bouquet in a large paper bag that kept it upright and secure, and covered it gently with a piece of tissue paper to keep the dust and sunlight off. It was then stored on top of a high bookshelf out of the way. The three bridesmaid bouquets were placed in a large covered box. They stood in glass jars, which meant that they stood at a slightly jaunty angle, but it was better than laying them down and squashing the petals.

Don't worry if some of your flowers do get a bit squashed. Crepe paper can be re-moulded quite easily with warm, dry hands. If you are brave enough, or the petals have become quite severely crushed, you can try ironing them out – but I would suggest this only as a last resort. Make sure the steam is switched off and the iron is on its lowest setting, as the water will cause the colours to run and stain, and a high temperature will burn the paper.

MAKE YOUR OWN GERBERA

This is one of the easiest flowers to make, and as each one has a relatively large surface area, you will need fewer of them to fill space. This is why I chose them for our buttonholes/ boutonnieres and corsages (see pages 46–48).

What you need

- ⊕ Gerbera petal template (page 124)
- ⊕ Paper-covered floristry wire, 18 gauge
- ⊕ Crepe paper:
    one black 6cm (2¼in) square per flower
    one 12 x 10cm (4¾ x 4in) strip and one
    50 x 6.5cm (20 x 2½in) strip per flower in the
    colour of your choice
- ⊕ Cotton wool ball or scrap of crepe paper
- ⊕ Green floristry tape
- ⊕ Pencil
- ⊕ Ruler
- ⊕ Scissors
- ⊕ Wire cutters
- ⊕ An old pillow (optional)

Instructions

1 Pinch off a piece of cotton wool or take a piece of scrap crepe paper and make it into a ball about 2cm (¾in) across. Place it in the centre of your black square of crepe paper.

2 Push the floral wire half way up into the cotton wool or crepe paper ball. Wrap the crepe paper square around the ball and gently twist the paper around the wire, taking care not to tear the paper or push the wire through it.

3 Place the pillow in your lap and rest the end of the wire against it. Wrap your floristry tape around the paper that is twisted onto the wire; start wrapping immediately underneath your ball of cotton wool or paper.

4 Continue wrapping the tape down the wire for about 5cm (2in). This will ensure it stays in place and is secure.

TIP:
TWISTING TECHNIQUE
If you hold the tape still but twist the wire stem against the pillow it is much easier to hold everything in place while still getting the tape tightly wrapped around the wire.

5 Take your 12 x 10cm (4¾ x 4in) coloured strip of crepe paper and fold it in half lengthways. Snip 4cm (1½in) long cuts into the open edge at 2–3mm (⅛in) intervals. It will start to look like a fringe.

6 Wind your fringed paper around the wire at the base of your black ball stamen, as shown.

7 Gradually pinch and concertina the fringe slightly as you wrap it. This will look more realistic and will also stop the layers of crepe sitting directly on top of each other, which can cause the paper to slip out of place once taped. You could experiment here by starting a little lower than shown, so that the fringe is just visible around the ball, then wrapping it gradually upwards so that it lifts up into longer fringes.

8 Once you are happy with your arrangement, tape it tightly in place. Wind the tape around the wire a few times and then, as before, gradually wind the tape down the wire for about 5cm (2in). Cut the tape off and put to one side.

9 Pick up your petal template and fold your long strip of crepe paper into a concertina the same width as your template. Try not to allow the crepe paper to stretch as you fold it.

10 Place your template on top of your folded paper and draw around the petal edges. Mark a dash on each end, as per the template; this indicates the depth of the petals.

TIP:
CLEAN UP
Regularly wash and dry your hands when using floral tape. It can get quite sticky, especially if your hands are warm, and can also transfer colour between the papers.

TIP:
PETAL PERFECTION
Remember that every flower will look ever so slightly different, so don't worry if you cut any of your paper strips slightly too long or too short. Use the paper anyway and just adjust how far you cut your fringe or petals to create a slightly smaller or larger bloom. Make use of as many oddments as you can. Don't waste your materials.

TIP:
PRODUCTION LINE

If you decide early on to make lots of one type of flower, organise yourself and break the making up process into stages. I would make twenty or more stamens in one go, cut out twenty lots of petals and then attach them all one after the other. It meant that I could get into the rhythm of each stage and wasn't constantly changing my tools and materials around.

11 Hold the folded layers of crepe paper very securely and cut around your pencil marks. Cut down between each petal as far as the pencil marks created in step 10. Take care that the layers do not slip by holding close to where you are cutting on each petal.

12 Open out the crepe paper length and cut down between each of the conjoined petals that sat at each end of your folded strip.

13 Pick up the strip of petals and very gently use your thumbs and forefingers to stretch out the end of each petal. Try not to tear them, but if any of them do rip, simply trim off the torn petal, as you won't notice that it is missing once the flower is made up.

14 Take your pencil and carefully roll all the petal ends around it, section by section; hold them in place for a few seconds and then release. They will look very curly at first but they will relax into a more natural bloom shape.

15 Pick up your stamen and place the end against the pillow on your lap. Place one end of the curled petal strip against where you attached the fringe, with the petals bending up and out. Gradually wind the petal length around the stamen and wire with a small pleat or pinch here and there so that the petals don't sit neatly on top of each other.

TIP:
PETAL PRACTICE

Be economical with your crepe paper oddments. If you find you have lots of left-over pieces, create a petal strip in two or three sections and attach them separately – no one will ever know.

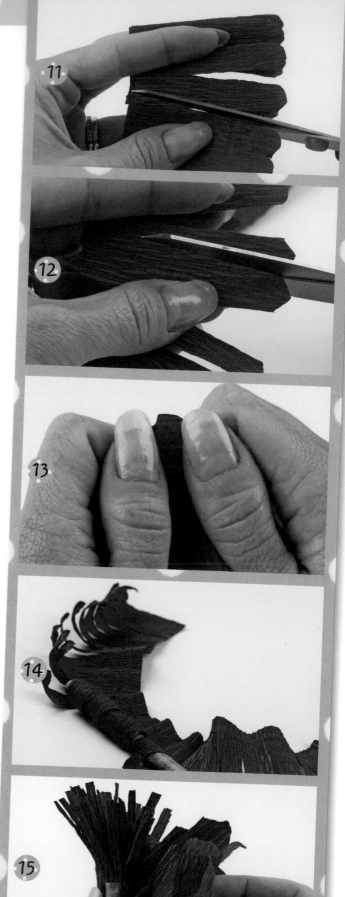

16 Keep checking the top of the flower to see how the petals are falling and adjust as you go. Pinch hard as you wind to keep it all together.

17 Once the full petal length is wound on and you are happy with the petal arrangement, use the floristry tape to tightly secure it in place.

18 Once you feel the flowerhead is secure, wind the tape about 10cm (4in) down the wire and cut.

TIP:
FUNKY FOLIAGE
I didn't create any foliage for my flowers, but if you want a leaf or two, cut some leaf shapes from green crepe paper and stretch and attach them in the same way as the petals.

MAKE YOUR OWN BUTTONHOLE/BOUTONNIERE

As my buttonholes/boutonnieres were gerberas, I've used one here. However, any flower can be used and made into a buttonhole/boutonniere by following the same method.

What you need

- ⊕ One ready-made paper flower, made using only half a length of paper-covered wire, see pages 42–45 or 86–95
- ⊕ Crepe paper: two 25cm x 15mm (10 x ²/₃in) strips of green
- ⊕ Green floristry tape
- ⊕ Pencil
- ⊕ Ruler
- ⊕ Scissors
- ⊕ 60cm (23½in) of 16mm (²/₃in) white satin-edged organza ribbon
- ⊕ Hot glue gun
- ⊕ Wire cutters

Instructions

1 Bend the flowerhead gently at 90 degrees, as shown.

2 Twist the two strips of green crepe paper between your fingers to form long, thin coils. Arrange them in two loops behind your gerbera (see finished example, above) and tape them into position using floristry tape. To get this right it may help to lay the flower against a flat surface, to mimic how it will appear when worn. They may look flimsy, but when secured on the flower and worn against a jacket they will sit correctly. Cut the wire stem to your desired length. I didn't cover the wires as they were barely visible beneath the flowers and against dark grey suits, but if you want to, now is a good time to do it. Perhaps use ribbon and secure it with hot glue.

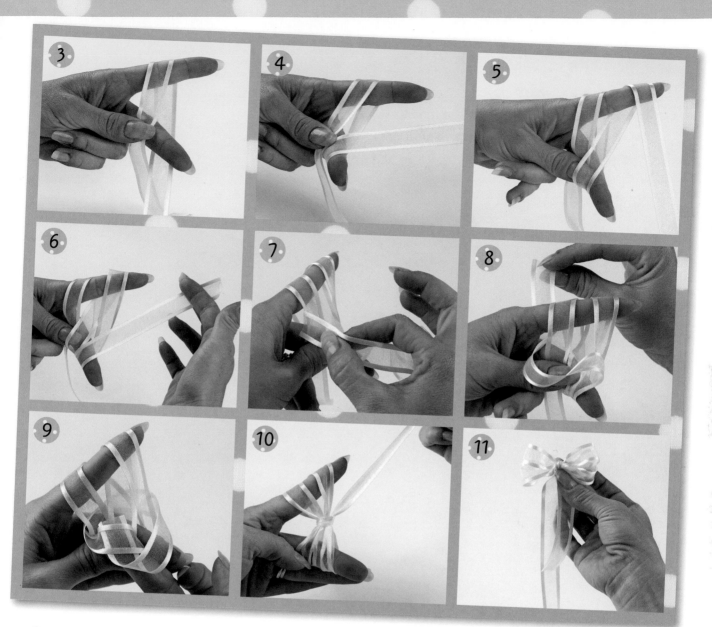

3 Separate your first two fingers into a 'V' shape, as shown. With your thumb, hold your ribbon length approximately 10cm (4in) up against your second finger, with the long tail of the ribbon hanging behind.

4 Bring the long tail of your ribbon under and then over your second finger, as shown.

5 Take the tail of ribbon up behind your first finger and then bring it down in front.

6 Again, bring the tail of the ribbon down under your second finger and then up in front, creating two loops on each finger.

7 Take the ribbon tail and feed it through the gap between your first and second fingers, from front to back.

8 Pull it all the way through to the back, as shown.

9 Bring the ribbon tail around the back of all the loops, and then bring it up through the start of this loop.

10 Pull it tight so it looks like a bow.

11 Slide the ribbon off your fingers and arrange it as you please. You can stick this to the stem using hot glue. When it has dried, cut the ribbon ends to the desired shape and length. Secure to the left lapel with a pin.

TIP:
FULL BOW
Create a triple bow by forming an extra figure-of-eight on your fingers before tying the knot.

MAKE YOUR OWN CORSAGE

I kept my ideas simple and made my corsages very similar to my buttonholes/boutonnieres. Corsages are usually larger, so I used two blooms instead of one. As an alternative, you could use coordinating ribbon to attach a flower to a guest's wrist instead, ensuring that you cover any sharp wire ends.

What you need

⊛ Two ready-made paper flowers, made using one length of paper-covered wire between both, see pages 42–45 or 86–95

⊛ Crepe paper: two 15cm x 15mm (6 x 2/3in) strips of green

⊛ Green floristry tape

⊛ Pencil

⊛ Ruler

⊛ Scissors

⊛ 60cm (23½in) of 16mm (2/3in) white satin-edged organza ribbon

⊛ Hot glue gun

Instructions

1 Bend the flowerheads gently at 90 degrees.

2 To ensure the flowers sit neatly together, place them on a flat surface and put one slightly below and to the right of the other. When you are happy with the arrangement, bend the stem of the lower flower to an angle of about 45 degrees, approximately 2–3cm (¾–1¼in) down from the head. Use floristry tape to stick both stems tightly together.

3 Twist the two strips of green crepe paper between your fingers to form long, thin coils. Arrange them in two loops behind your flowers and tape them into position using floristry tape. To get this right it may help to lay the flowers against a flat surface, to mimic how the corsage will appear when worn.

4 Cut the wire stems to your desired length. I didn't cover the wires of my corsages, but if you want to, now is a good stage to do it. Perhaps use ribbon and secure it with hot glue.

5 To make and attach a bow to your corsage, follow steps 3–11 on page 47.

MAKE YOUR OWN BOUQUET

Once you have mastered the gerbera flower technique, making a bouquet couldn't be simpler. You can adapt the handle length and the colours really easily so that it matches your colour scheme.

What you need

- ✪ Thirteen ready-made paper flowers, see pages 42–45 or 86–95
- ✪ Ten pearl-headed pins
- ✪ Hot glue gun
- ✪ 1m (39in) pink raffia
- ✪ Scissors
- ✪ 2–3m (78–117in) of 16mm (²⁄₃in) white satin-edged organza ribbon, plus extra for the bow
- ✪ 2–3m (78–117in) string

1 You will need to arrange your flowers into a 'ball' or 'circle' arrangement. This will require you to bend the stems at varying angles and heights, as shown, to create a pleasing, even arrangement.

2 Tie string around the stems to keep them in place. Leaving a gap of about 2cm (¾in) free at either end, cover the length tightly with string and tie it off.

3 Cover the entire length of the stems with white ribbon; secure it at the top with a pin or hot glue then wind it down the entire length. Use pins or hot glue to secure and hide the end.

4 Pin one end of the length of raffia at the top of the stem. Tightly, and with even, open spacing, wrap it down the stem and pin it in place at the bottom. Once secured, bring it back up the stem, winding in the same way to create a criss-cross pattern. Pin the end in place at the top of the stem. Pin the raffia in place at each criss-cross, using pearl-headed pins to make an attractive feature. To make and attach a bow to your bouquet, follow steps 3–11 on page 47, creating three loops around your fingers at step 4; leave long flowing ribbon ends for an elegant effect. If you want lots of dangling ribbons, tie another long length of ribbon around the middle of the bow.

STITCHED ACCESSORIES

Why not make some beautiful stitched items for your wedding party? There are plenty of ways to save money and create some stunning fabric accessories. The key, as always, is to keep it simple. You don't even have to make things from scratch – adjust, modify and tweak bought items to bring them in line with your theme.

From scratch

For example, if you want the men's pocket squares in a specific fabric but are unable to hire them, you could easily make them by hand. If you are having a vintage wedding, floral pocket squares would look wonderful. All you'd need to do is cut a square of fabric and neatly hem all four edges by hand or with a sewing machine. Or, if you are careful with your fabric choice, you could use pinking shears for a zigzagged edge to save on sewing. There are lots of ideas online for fabric hair accessories, too. You can make some really simple flowers, rosettes and abstract shape decorations, which could tie in with the style and theme. You could even decorate your shoes with a fabric accessory.

Adjusting, modifying and tweaking

Our bridesmaids wore white, shop-bought elasticated belts. White went well with their dresses and also matched my dress. To separate the best woman from my bridesmaids I wanted her to wear a dark grey belt so that she matched the grey of the groomsmen's suits. Could I find a matching grey elasticated belt anywhere? No! In the end I bought a grey belt with a very elaborate butterfly clasp and an extra white one, and interchanged the clasps with a touch of cutting and sewing.

Adapt your stitched accessories like my experiment here. I have used the same template for the blue flower above but used a lilac organza. It is great to experiment with different fabrics as you will find they all have different results.

MAKE YOUR OWN VEIL

How about doing as I did and making your own veil? I tried one on in a bridal shop and really liked it, but really disliked the price tag. Mum saw how simple it was and went out and constructed one almost immediately from tulle for a fraction of the price. We discovered it was called a 'bubble' veil. The one in the shop had little diamantés scattered around the base of it, but when I tried on my own veil at a dress fitting I decided simplicity was best and that I didn't need the extra sparkles. Here's how to make it…

What you need

- ✪ 1.5m (1²/₃ yd) length of white tulle
- ✪ White cotton thread
- ✪ Pins
- ✪ Needle
- ✪ Transparent hair comb accessory

Instructions

1 Fold your piece of tulle in half along the longest edge. Pin the two short ends together, spacing your pins about 30cm (12in) apart.

2 Sew a neat running stitch approximately 5mm (¼in) down from the top edge, across the width of both layers of tulle; gather it as you go.

3 When you reach the end, check how tightly gathered the tulle is – this will dictate how rounded the veil will be. If it is too tight, loosen it a little. Secure the end of the thread by sewing back through a few layers of tulle.

4 You can now position the veil onto the underside of the hair comb, as shown. Secure the layers of tulle to the first tooth of the comb by stitching around it several times.

5 Stitch through the layers of gathered tulle and up through each tooth of the comb two or three times to make sure it is secure.

6 To position the veil correctly, hold it in front of you, as shown, and run it down over the back of your head, into your hair, with the curve of the comb following the curve of your head (the veil will be hanging down over your face). Flip the veil back over your head to finish.

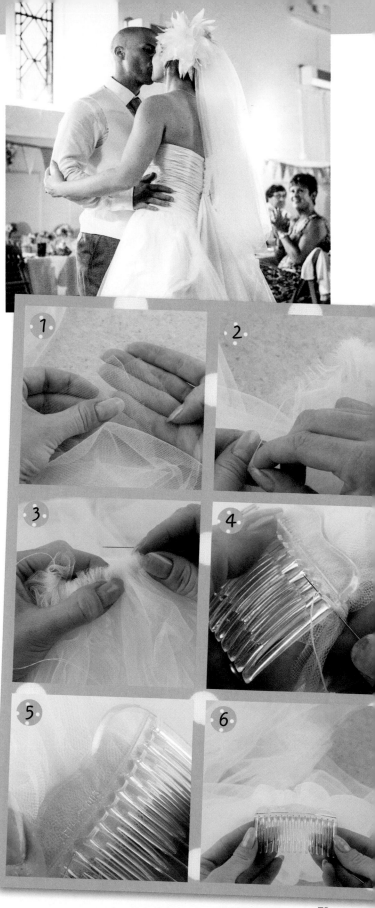

MAKE YOUR OWN HAIR FLOWER

I didn't want to go down the traditional route of wearing a sparkly tiara. As most of the wedding was flower-themed, I decided to extend it to all the hair decorations for the bridal party. I found some images online that I fell in love with. Initially, my mum and I tried making a hair flower from silk taffeta, but the fabric was very stiff and didn't sit quite right. We tried again with polyester organza, which matched one of the fabrics in my wedding dress and was gorgeously delicate and fragile. I couldn't resist the soft, fraying results it gave. Follow the instructions given, right, to make one for yourself. If you are unsure about the size, or want a practice run, experiment with a cheaper fabric, such as cotton, first.

What you need

- ✪ Flower hair template (page 126)
- ✪ Polyester organza, 30cm (12in) by the width of the fabric
- ✪ White cotton thread
- ✪ Large hair snap clip
- ✪ Scissors
- ✪ Needle
- ✪ Pins
- ✪ Spray stiffening agent (optional)

TIP: ADAPTING TO SUIT

Cut the depth of your strip from a whole fabric width. Follow the instructions, and when you are satisfied with the fullness of your flower, cut off the excess. This gives you complete control over how full you want the flower. If you are brave enough, you can use this offcut to start making another flower and then join the next strip onto this. This will make the most of the fabric you have, which could save you some money if you are making several flowers. For smaller flowers, use half the fabric width.

Instructions

1 Cut out the flower hair template. Fold your piece of organza in half lengthways, so that the two long edges meet. Then fold the fabric into a concertina the same width as the template. Pin all the layers together.

2 Cut the petal shapes through all the layers. Make sure the flat edge of the template sits on the folded fabric edge. Hold tightly near to where you are cutting, to stop the fabric from slipping too much.

3 Cut a long length of cotton thread and double it for extra strength. Tie a knot in the end and begin to sew a running stitch approximately 5mm (¼in) from the folded fabric edge. Sew along and gradually gather the stitches together by pulling the fabric along your stitches.

4 Start to roll the gathered edge into a circle, securing with a few stitches as you go.

5 Continue to gather the fabric and roll the gathers into the circle.

6 Secure the completed circle with a few stitches.

7 Sew the flower to the snap hair clip. Do this by sewing loops of cotton thread through sections of the clip and back through the fabric.

8 Manipulate the petals into position and snip any odd bits that you think might need tidying. Dangle your flower upside down and gently spray stiffening agent onto it if you wish. Do it gradually so as not to oversaturate and solidify the fabric!

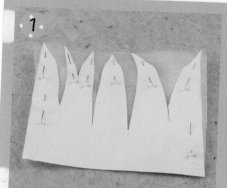

1

2

3

4

5

6

7

8

TIP:
WHICH CLIP?
You could attach your flower to any type of hair clip, comb or accessory. If you are having a complicated hair do then talk to your stylist about what clip would work best. Also think about the type of hair you have: for smooth silky hair you will need a clip that will snap shut or has teeth on it to grip your hair.

Bridesmaids

I used the same flower, but smaller, for my bridesmaids and best woman. They were all made using a lightweight poly-cotton. The bridesmaids' turquoise blue flowers were made from off-cuts that I requested from the company that made two of the bridesmaid dresses, and the best woman's grey flower came from off-cuts from the bottom of my dad's suit trousers. Both were made in exactly the same way, using the smaller template on page 126. Cut a strip of fabric 15cm (6in) by half the fabric width, and follow the instructions, above. If you are planning on making a smaller version, perhaps for buttonholes/boutonnieres or for a flower girl's hair decoration, do a practice run with the larger one first as this is much easier to make if you only have very basic sewing skills. You'll pick up the techniques more easily and then you'll be much more competent when making the smaller version.

THE CEREMONY

Although the ceremony is the shortest part of the wedding day, it is by far the most important. It is the focus of the whole occasion and possibly the most photographed portion of the day, so you want to make sure it looks stunning. The ceremony is the time where you, as the bride, make your grand entrance in front of your husband-to-be and all your treasured guests, so the venue has got to complement you and make you feel confident and relaxed.

PERSONALISING YOUR SPACE

Whether you are marrying in a church, registry office or licenced venue, you need to check what decoration is permitted. Ensure you're clear on exactly what you can and can't do, and talk to the management about health and safety restrictions. For example, they may not allow paper decorations like mine if you plan on having candles as well!

Visit the venue as many times as you feel necessary. Measure up the spaces where you might put flowers or other decorations. The advantage to being a DIY bride is that everything you make is made to order, so go and measure every space you think you can use. Take photographs of the space from each angle. This will give you a visual record of what is there. Make a note of what can be removed or added. Don't forget to look up – decorations can be hung from up high. Draw out a visual map of the decorations that are required. Ask lots of questions and perhaps see if you can visit on the morning of a wedding to see what others have achieved, and to see what inspiration you can take from it.

If you are having the ceremony and reception at different venues, consider what can be doubled up as decoration for both. Pew ends can be transported from the church and hung on the back of chairs at your reception to inject an extra splash of colour. The windowsill arrangements of a registry office could be reused. If the logistics of transporting decorations and setting them up again is not too difficult, this could save you a lot of time and money.

Things to think about...

1. What items do you need?
Look at the space you have and think about how to spruce it up. Do you want flowers? Would you prefer bunting or leafy garlands? The choices are never ending so, as always, do your research and take inspiration from others. Measure the spaces you want to fill and take pictures for future reference. If you decide to make your own confetti, you need to decide what to store and display it in, so that your guests can use it. Is that an extra item you need to make? Sit down and make a long wishlist and see what is essential before you start making.

2. How many items do you need?
This will depend on your wishlist. Some venues – churches in particular – can seem like an overwhelming space to fill, so think about using large decorations, such as oversized paper pompoms, which you'll need fewer of. Tiny, delicate detail will be lost when items are put into a large space, so get your impact from size, colour or pattern rather than detail.

3. When are the items needed by?
This is entirely up to you and depends on the amount of forward planning you want to do. The ceremony decorations were the items that I made first. It is the most significant part of the day so it had to be right. I made my decorations months in advance, took them to the church and tried and tested them in situ to make sure I was happy with the presence they had. If you also decide to plan far ahead, remember to find somewhere you can store the items.

4. How much can you afford to spend?
The bigger your venue, the more there is to decorate. Perhaps come up with a design that is minimal and simple. Or perhaps you could be creative with your materials and decorate your venue with real flowers, freshly cut from the gardens of your friends and family. Recycling your decorations is also a good way to cut costs. Use the same arrangements at the reception and borrow what you can from friends.

Setting up and taking down

Check when you are allowed into your venue to decorate. We had the whole day before our wedding to set up, but there was a couple marrying in the church the day after us, so they had to wait for us to get married and to dismantle before they could decorate for their day. We gave this job to our groomsmen and bridesmaids while our guests made their way to the reception.

Other considerations

Some venues won't allow confetti unless it is organic and biodegradable. If this is the case with yours, why not seize the opportunity and make your own from dried petals?

Consider making items such as a ring pillow for the ring bearer or reading cards for guests who are presenting a poem or reading during the ceremony.

PAPER POMPOMS

I absolutely love paper pompoms. They bring huge amounts of colour to a room or outdoor space with very little effort. They are soft enough to be elegant as well as fun and are super cheap. They are also very simple to make, so hopefully you'll be able to get friends and family involved in the creation process. As always, do plenty of research – there are lots of crafters out there who have fashioned all sorts of variations on the basic theme, and I found several that took my fancy.

How I used them. . .

St Mary's Church isn't enormous, but due to the high ceilings and minimal décor it appeared to be a huge space to fill. These pompoms really did the job. As you can see, I made three different sizes of pompom. I used one of each strung together vertically in different colour sequences as pew ends. They were only half opened so that they laid against the surface neatly. If you go for something similar, make sure that they don't become a play thing for young children – ensure that the groomsmen are keeping a protective eye out on the day!

I created four windowsill arrangements using the three different sizes, arranging them in some dry oasis/floral foam that had been taped together with floristry tape. I also produced three arrangements for the entrance porch of the church. These were similar to the windowsill arrangements, but not quite so large. There were also two very small arrangements for the altar, and one huge arrangement for the pedestal at the front. The pedestal in particular was a challenge. I measured the stand and took pictures before I started. I had to guess a height I thought would look good and create a carved dry oasis/floral foam base, stuck together with floristry tape. This enabled me to push my pompom wires into it all the way to the top.

I had no training for these arrangements; I simply researched real church flower arrangements and made them up as I went along, based on what I thought looked good. Trying them in situ long before the wedding also enabled me to make any slight adjustments with time to spare.

TIP:
STUCK UP

Check with your venue about how your pompoms can be attached – you can't just stick things up with tape or sticking putty as it might ruin old, valuable furniture!

TIP:
HIGH WIRE

If you are going to make floral arrangements, leave the wires long so that you can push them into your oasis/floral foam. You can trim the ends if necessary when creating your arrangements.

MAKE YOUR OWN PAPER POMPOMS

Here are the basic instructions for making a paper pompom. Once you've got the hang of this, you can adapt it to create all the variations you want (see pages 62–63).

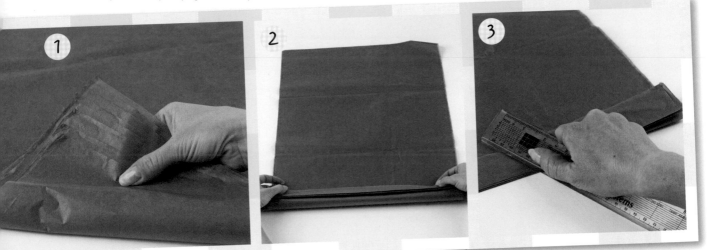

Instructions

1 The method for making pompoms is the same no matter what size you are making; here I am making a large pompom, with eight sheets of paper. Layer your eight sheets of tissue paper directly on top of one another

2 Make concertina folds into the shorter side at 3.5cm (1¼in) intervals. If you are making a medium-sized pompom make the folds 2cm (¾in) wide; for a small pompom make the folds 1cm (½in) wide.

3 Use your ruler to flatten each fold as you go – this will make it less bulky when you come to cut the petals.

TIP:
FILL OUT
If you're fully opening out the pompoms, use more sheets of tissue: use 10–12 sheets for large pompoms, 8–10 sheets for medium-sized pompoms and 6–8 sheets for small pompoms.

TIP:
DRY OFF
Make sure your hand are dry.

4 Draw around your circular item at each end of your concertina to make a petal shape. Use sharp scissors to cut through all the layers of paper. Make sure you hold the layers tightly so they don't slip; you may find it helps to lay something heavy on top of the paper to prevent the layers slipping.

5 Fold your concertina in half to find the middle. Bend a length of floristry wire about one-third of the way down and manipulate it around the middle of the concertina, twisting it around itself to secure.

6 Lay the paper on its side and fan out both ends. Bend the excess wire at 90 degrees. Separate the layers of tissue by gently teasing them with your fingers from the tip to as near to the centre fold as possible.

7 Open all eight layers up towards you to create half-opened pompoms. Don't panic if one or two of the tips tear as they aren't likely to be noticed if you trim them off neatly.

8 Once opened out, the tissue can be manipulated to make sure the folds are evenly spread out and the central wire is hidden.

TIP:
SHARPEN UP
You will need to use really strong scissors to be able to cut through all the layers of your pompom. I used sharpened dressmaker's scissors, which shouldn't normally be used with paper, but it was necessary to snip through the bulk.

ALTERNATIVE POMPOM IDEAS

There are lots of imaginative ways to transform a basic pompom into something magnificent. Why not try making them in several different sizes, so that you can use them to decorate different parts of your venue? You could open them out fully and hang them from the ceiling – which looks fabulous in a white marquee – or you could leave them half opened; the flat side can then be positioned against doors, gates or chairs. They also look fabulous like this because they appear much fuller in volume. As a splash of colour for the table, why not tie up your cutlery with miniature pompoms, or place a pompom on top of a boxed favour.

Pompom centrepieces

Here's an idea for your table centrepieces. Make medium-size pompoms but add extra layers of tissue to make them appear fuller when opened into a full bloom. Try cutting the petals with pinking shears to make them look a bit different. Place them in decorative candle holders filled with white stones in the bottom to help weigh them down and hold them in place (shop around – consider buying fish tank stones as these are cheaper than decorative stones). Alternatively, dry oasis/floral foam in the very bottom will help the pompoms stand upright, but you will also need to add some weight to stop them toppling over.

Pompom garland

String fully opened pompoms along a piece of decorative ribbon and hang them up like bunting. When you are making them, tie around the middles with string rather than wire, as the pompoms will hang more naturally. Leave a long tail of string to hang each pompom with – once the pompom is opened it will be almost impossible to try and attach another piece of string to it! A pompom garland could also look beautiful hung along the front of the top table.

Pompom table runner

If you are short on table space, this attractive runner could be a good solution. Make lots of the smallest size pompoms and hot glue them onto a length of ribbon, leaving a long length spare at each end to hang stylishly off the end of a table. Make a double bow (following the directions on page 47) with extra long ribbon ends, to help finish it off.

Alternative pompom petals

To create variety among your pompoms, cut different shapes into the ends of the folded paper before opening them out. Try one single quarter curve so that each fold looks like a giant petal, or cut double curves to create a more decorative effect (number 2). Try cutting points (number 1) or even double points (number 5) for a more dramatic effect. Just be aware that the pointed cuts are a little harder to open out and are more prone to tearing. Consider cutting the ends with pinking shears (number 4) or snipping into the ends (number 3) for an alternative look. Also try layering several different colours of tissue paper together to create a variegated flower (number 6), or add extra layers of tissue to make your pompoms appear even fuller.

Petal types

1. Single point
2. Double petal
3. Snipped edge
4. Pinking shear point
5. Double point
6. Variegated

1.

2.

3.

4.

5.

6.

MAKE YOUR OWN RING PILLOW

A ring pillow is not a must-have for every wedding. Traditionally you would only use one if you have a ring bearer. A ring bearer is usually a young male relative or close friend between the ages of four and ten who walks down the aisle in front of the bride carrying the rings. However, these days couples often have girls or even pets carrying the rings to the vicar or registrar; other couples choose not to have a ring bearer at all. If you do decide to have a ring bearer, a ring pillow highlights the importance of the rings tied to it, so it can be a beautiful and elegant addition to your decoration.

TIP:
MAKE IT YOURS

Make this project more personal and change the colours of the ribbons to be his and hers, or perhaps change the colour of the flower or the pillow to match your dress or the other decorations that will be on show. You could even glam it up with a few little diamantés sewn onto the edges of the petals. For a fuller flower effect, add more petals to the top flower.

What you need

- ⊕ 50cm (19¾in) silk taffeta
- ⊕ Cotton thread
- ⊕ Toy stuffing
- ⊕ Two 30cm (12in) lengths of 3mm (⅛in) wide white satin ribbon
- ⊕ Pinking shears
- ⊕ Scissors
- ⊕ Tape measure
- ⊕ Needle
- ⊕ 15cm (6in) square of fusible interfacing
- ⊕ Iron

Instructions

1 Cut a strip of taffeta measuring 30 x 15cm (12 x 6in). Fuse your interfacing onto the wrong side of one end of your taffeta strip – ensure that it is set to the right temperature for the fabric, so as not to burn it. This creates a stable top side of the ring pillow, which will make it easier to sew through.

2 With pinking shears, cut seven 9 x 19cm (3½ x 7½in) rectangles and two 6 x 13cm (2½ x 5in) rectangles from the taffeta, rounding the corners as you go.

3 Fold each petal in half to find the centre point, then sew a gathering stitch across the width; gather the thread to pinch in the centre to create a petal-like appearance. Sew through the centre a few times to secure the 'petals' in place.

4 Put four large petals to one side. Sew the three remaining large petals into the centre of the interfaced section of taffeta, right side up. Do this one at a time, layering them at different angles, to create a star-like flower.

5 Sew the two small petals in alternating directions to form a cross shape on top of the three large petals. Arrange them in a way that the petals don't sit directly on top of one another but cross over the joins to make it look more realistic.

6 The remaining four petals can now be sewn onto each corner of the pillow, as shown, approximately 5cm (2in) in from the corner point.

7 Fold your ribbon lengths in half and position them in the centre of the flower. Secure each in the centre with a few stitches, ready for your rings to be tied on.

8 Fold the pillow base in half and neatly hand sew two edges together using over-edge stitch; fold the pillow edges inwards slightly to neaten as you sew.

9 Stuff the pillow until plump with toy stuffing, then sew up the third edge to complete.

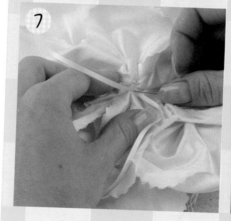
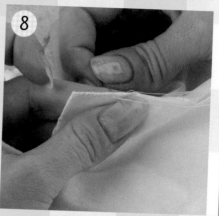

LEAVING THE CEREMONY

Leaving the ceremony as a newly married couple is really exciting, and it was important to us to get some shots straight afterwards. And what better opportunity than with a good old-fashioned confetti throwing shot? I should think that all guests enjoy cheering and throwing confetti over a newly wedded couple, however, having been to many weddings myself, confetti seems to be the one thing I always forget to take. It can also be a bit of a potential minefield, as many wedding venues won't allow anything other than natural or biodegradable petals, which can be quite expensive to buy. I really wanted a confetti throwing picture for our wedding album and saw it as part of the tradition. I decided to make our own confetti, for free! I also made paper cones to keep it in and upcycled an old fruit box to store it (see pages 68–71).

You'll need to think about any decorations you might like outside. I created a few extra pompoms to decorate the church door, and also strung a 3m (10ft) garland around the gate where we were doing the confetti throwing, to ensure that our colourful theme carried through to the outdoor photographs.

If you have a wedding car, think about using the bouquets as flower arrangements for the back shelf. If you are holding your reception at a different location and want to re-use some of your decorations, this is the ideal opportunity to start moving some of these items, as people will be departing for the reception.

TIP:
WEATHER WATCH
Keep an eye on the weather forecast the day before your wedding as paper flowers won't survive outside in the rain or severe wind and can bleed their colour, which will cause staining.

String of pompoms

This garland gate decoration was easy to make and turned out to be really beautiful. It provided a stunning colourful back drop for the confetti throwing shots. If you make your own, follow the instructions on page 60 and make sure your excess wire sticks out at 90 degrees to the flat side of your pompom. Bend it into a loop and twist the ends in. You can then tie string to these loops to join them.

TIP:
BE LOCATION WISE
Think about opportunities for photographs after the ceremony. It's the most important part of the day and where you, as the bride, will look your freshest. Keep an eye on the weather, as this can have a huge impact on your photographs: have back-up ideas for indoor locations, and make sure they are decorated as you want to remember them.

MAKE YOUR OWN CONFETTI

If you are going to make your own confetti, be sure to plan ahead and work out when the flowers you want are in bloom. Roses are the traditional choice – and different varieties will flower from the spring and summer months right through until autumn – but I found that most small blooms worked well.

When sourcing paper to make cones, think about where you can get it for free; much of mine came from the free inserts you get with card-making magazines. I was lucky to be surrounded by an abundance of them at work, but see if any crafty friends or family members have any. Also go to your local DIY store and pick up some wallpaper samples. They won't be patterned on both sides but will be strong and durable. Brown packaging paper can be quite cheap too and can make a beautiful vintage-style cone. You could also print a pattern onto plain printer paper.

I customised my own box to hold the cones in place for easy distribution to my guests. If you don't want to take the project this far, the cones could just be popped in a basket, as long as there are enough of them to support one another.

Instructions: confetti

1 Lay a few sheets of kitchen roll on a tray and spread out the petals in a thin layer.

2 Place them in a warm, dry place. Check on them each day and within two to three days they will have dried and become crispy.

3 Store them until needed in plastic food bags. Ensure they are completely dry first, or they will rot.

4 Do this in batches until you have the required amount.

TIP:
LAYER UP
You can layer up your petals on the tray between pieces of kitchen towel. They will take a little longer to dry but if there is no rush, it is worth doing.

TIP:
GIVING CONFETTI THE BRUSH OFF

When the confetti lands on you, be sure to brush it off fairly promptly, as if you get hot the natural colourings can leak out and permanently stain your clothing.

What you need

For the paper cones:

⊕ Several sheets of 15cm (6in) square patterned or coloured paper: if possible, use paper that is patterned on both sides

⊕ 1cm (½in) wide double-sided tape

⊕ Scissors

⊕ Ruler

⊕ Pencil

For the box holder:

⊕ An old fruit box or a cheap wooden tray

⊕ Toilet roll cardboard tubes

⊕ White paint

⊕ Hot glue gun

Instructions: paper cones

1 Turn your 15cm (6in) paper squares so that the right side is face down on your table. Place a strip of double-sided tape down one edge of the square and fold it over by 1cm (½in) to stick it down. This will provide a neat outside edge when the paper is rolled up into a cone. On the folded edge, place another piece of double-sided tape.

2 Pull two of the opposite corners together and let the taped edge run down the outside edge as you roll it into a cone shape.

3 Tease and pinch the point of the cone and stick it in place by peeling off the double-sided tape. You will now have a beautiful paper cone.

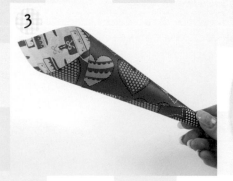

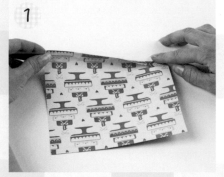

TIP:
CONE STYLE
You could add extra decoration to these cones, such as diamantés or pieces of ribbon, or even pieces of card with your names written on, stuck across the join line with double-sided tape. Remember though, that these will get thrown away, so don't spend too long on them.

Instructions: box holder

1 Cut the toilet roll tubes in half until you have enough of them to fill your box. Paint them and the box white or in the colours of your choice.

2 Once the paint has dried, use a hot glue gun to apply glue to the bottom edge of each tube.

3 Stick the tubes to the base of your box in an upright position.

4 Once dried, stand a cone in each tube. Consider making a sign to stick to the side of the box. Think about the styling used for your invitations and other stationery and create something that continues the 'theme'; I used the same colours, fonts and printed embellishments.

TIP:

TIME IT RIGHT

Leave it until the last possible moment to fill the cones with your confetti as it could tip out or blow away in the breeze. I filled mine the day before the wedding and took them to be stored at the church.

4

CONFETTI

THE RECEPTION

The reception was the biggest feat of my imagination and the most enjoyable part of my wedding planning. I had a huge blank canvas, indoors and out, to decorate however I wished.

I must be honest and say there were moments when I didn't think I could achieve what I wanted and became very overwhelmed with the scale not only of what I was making, but also the practicalities of the day. I had to pre-plan a lot of the wedding day timetable and rely on a lot of other people to keep it all running smoothly – and in the end, it did.

The most important thing is to plan the room as an interior designer would. Make the most of the space you have and re-use some of that space for the evening if you need to. My advice would be to make the space bright, inviting and practical for your guests. Include some entertainment for children and provide a seating plan so that your guests can easily find their way to their seats.

Things to think about…

1. What items do you need?
Look back at the plan you made for your room and make a list of everything you need. Work out what items you need to buy, make or hire, and work out if there are any items you need to start collecting, such as old jars or bottles to use as vases, or petals for making table confetti.

2. How many items do you need?
Measure your tables and try to judge what you want to fit in that space: consider everything that might be there, such as your favours, place names, cutlery, glassware, wine, water and your centrepiece. Try to work out all the quantities in advance. If you can buy your supplies in bulk, it often saves on cost, particularly shipping.

3. When are the items needed by?
Essentially the day before the wedding, but you probably don't want to leave it that late! The day before your wedding will ideally be your set-up day. You need plenty of time for that, as items such as bunting can take longer than expected to put up. You want to have contingency time in case anything is left behind or you fall into any unexpected problems. Save your table plan until last.

4. How much can you afford to spend?
If you choose to make a lot of items yourself, this can be one of the most affordable parts of your day. Look at local market stalls for cheap supplies of fabric and paper. You don't necessarily need luxury items for many of the crafts, as people will not notice the difference. Lanterns can be made from old tin cans and wine bottles can be used as vases. Also remember to ask around your friends and family for bunting or other items you can borrow.

FILLING YOUR SPACE

The advantage to decorating the reception venue yourself is that you can make as much or as little as you like. You will be able to find lots of items to buy or hire in stores or online if you don't fancy making them, or if you run out of time.

If, as I did, you have a complete blank canvas and have decided to create everything from scratch, you are going to need a lot of time, patience and help from those around you. You'll need to have a clear vision of what you want to achieve.

Sometimes the best way to do this is to try and mock up what you want to see. For instance, mock up a table layout at home with your selection of items to check that you like the colour scheme and to check the spacing. Search online for photographers' galleries of photographs from your wedding venue: you may find that these help you visualise what works and what doesn't and give you ideas you hadn't considered.

Spatial decorations

Depending on your venue, you may want decorations to break up areas of white or empty space and to add a lovely splash of colour and sense of celebration. Bunting is perfect for this and has become very popular over recent years. It can transform both inside and outside areas, and is particularly good for spaces with high ceilings. Large paper pompoms, paper lanterns, fold-out paper stars, curtains of crepe paper ribbons or even swathes of fabric similar to the inside of a marquee, can also turn a boring or plain room into something that looks special. Period venues, such as barns or country houses, may lend themselves to sympathetic swathes of hops, ivy or flowers. Make sure you check whether your venue has any restrictions regarding hanging items, or any other health and safety issues.

Table decorations

If you want to spend some time crafting something beautiful, elegant and highly detailed then do it with your table decorations. When seated, your guests will spend an awful lot of time looking at these elements, so surprise them with something spectacular. Most of the items are necessary and serve a purpose, but think about taking those standard elements and making them a little bit different with something extraordinary and personal. Make vases out of old bottles or spray paint some tin cans and tie ribbon and lace around them. It's inexpensive and can look really pretty.

Additional decorations

There are always extra bits and pieces you can add to the reception to make it function better, or just to be indulgent. I wanted a cake stall for guests to eat from after the main meal, so as well as the wedding cake, I asked a few guests to make and bring some cakes and cookies to fill up the table. They were really popular, as was the candy stall, with adults and children alike. You can also be really creative with your boxes for cards or gifts, your tableplan and your guestbook. If you are having an outdoor wedding, why not supply a box of blankets for guests in the evening, or a box of sandals for guests who need a break from their high heels.

Personalisation is the key to creating something totally different to all the other weddings you have attended. I crafted a chalkboard with our wedding date on it and a timetable of the day so that our guests knew what was happening. You could create something similar but instead of writing your timetable on it, ask guests to write their best wishes to you both. Spray the board with clear varnish the following day and you will have a beautiful wall hanging to cherish for many years to come.

HOW I DID IT: BUNTING

Our village hall was Victorian with very high windows and a pitched roof, which left a huge expanse of white wall at eye-level. Adding colourful, patterned bunting to these areas brought the hall to life and created a sense of celebration.

Bunting was one of the most time-consuming crafts of our wedding. In fact we needed so much of it, my parents had to take over the making of it so that we could get it all done. My parents joined me when I first visited the village hall with my drawn plans. I had already been to measure up the outside spaces, hedgerows, fences and lamp posts; just about anywhere it could be tied to, and had roughly drawn a to-scale image of those features with my lines of bunting. I then returned to measure where my strings would attach to ensure I made the correct amounts. During this visit my parents saw a far better way of hanging the bunting at the front of the hall, so it was just as well they came with me. We were also able to check which beams we could hang it from inside the building and check what rules we had to adhere to.

Once I had my measurements, I was able to properly total up the amount of bunting I needed. It came to 300m (984¼ft)! Next I drew up a triangle template that was big enough to have an impact when hung high up in the beams. I then roughly guessed how far apart I wanted the pennants on the string, which enabled us to work out how many would be needed for the entire length and, in turn, approximately how much fabric I would need.

I scoured local stores, markets and online fabric stores for good deals on fabrics, and decided that our local market was the best place. My mum knew the stall holder quite well, so he gave us a good discount on several colours and patterns of fabric, which took me a good hour to choose.

When it came to hanging the bunting, we decided to use pieces of string tied to the ribbon ends. Ribbon is often quite slippery and can lose grip when tied up, particular when it is supporting the weight of lots of fabric. String was also a lot slimmer than the ribbon I used, so it could be fed through tiny spaces, or wound around nails to be tied up neatly.

Most of the bunting was made to the correct size for the inside of the building – this was scrupulously measured – but on the outside, my mum just kept adding the pennants onto the ribbon, until the ribbon ran out. This meant it could be cut to size onsite as we put it up.

It became quite a spectacle in the sleepy village over that weekend, causing lots of people to stop and ask what was happening. When I first saw it hung up outside I was quite overwhelmed by the impact it had, which was far better than I had imagined.

What you need

- A4 (8¼ x 11¾in) paper
- Sturdy template card
- Sewing machine
- Pinking shears, or rotary cutter with pinking shear disc, cutting mat and safety ruler (see tip, below right)
- Measuring stick
- To create 300m (984¼ft) you will need about 40m (131¼ft) of fabric – you can divide this amount over several different fabrics if you wish: I chose six
- 300m (984¼ft) of 23mm (1in) grosgrain ribbon in a colour of your choice
- Cotton sewing thread

MAKE YOUR OWN BUNTING

Use bunting to bring colour and life to your reception venue. Bunting is a great space-filler and is really easy to make – it is usually positioned so high up that you can make it single-sided, as guests won't notice the wrong side of the fabric. Here I will give you some directions and tips on how to make it in large quantities. You must measure your room space carefully to make sure you create the right length: total up the amount of fabric you need by working out how many triangles you will have on your length of bunting and work out how many you can cut from a width of fabric. To create your pennant template, fold an A4 (8¼ x 11¾in) piece of paper in half lengthways. Draw a diagonal line from the bottom left corner to the top right, and cut along this. Transfer this triangular pennant shape onto a piece of card, as this will be sturdy and therefore accurate with repeated use.

TIP: SEW UNIQUE

If you are short of time, why not email a few close friends or family and send them the task of making a certain length of bunting each? You can specify your colour scheme and you will get a lovely mix of all sorts of individual looking bunting. I made a length for a friend's wedding and really enjoyed the task.

TIP: FINDING FABRICS

To keep costs down, use up old scraps of fabric from friends and family, or cut up some old shirts, tablecloths or curtains. This could create a wonderful vintage style.

TIP: QUICK CUTS

If, like I did, you are going to make hundreds of metres of bunting to fill up your space, it may be worth investing in a rotary cutter, cutting mat and large ruler. A rotary cutter is like a pizza cutter for fabric, which means you can cut through several layers at a time and will create more accurate straight lines than with scissors; they are often used by quilters or patchworkers. Ask around and see if anyone has one you can borrow, and buy fresh blades for a good sharp cut.

Instructions

1 Draw around your card pennant template onto the back of your fabrics. Create minimal waste by alternating the direction of the pennant shape each time, so that the point is either at the top or the bottom, and the long sides touch. This should create a slanted square shape, which means less cutting and much less waste. If you are using a rotary cutter, you can layer several pieces of fabric.

2 Stack your pennants in the pattern or colour order of your choice. This will ensure your pattern repeats correctly.

3 Pin your first six pennants on the ribbon in the correct pattern order with approximately a 2.5cm (1in) gap between each one, making sure the right sides are facing down.

4 Using a zigzag stitch on your sewing machine, sew your pennants onto the ribbon approximately 1cm (½in) from the bottom edge. Continue repeating your pattern in this way. Once you get more confident you may not need to pin the pennants before sewing them, which would save valuable time.

TIP:
MEASURE FOR MEASURE
To keep tabs on your progress, measure your bunting length as you sew, using either a garden cane, stick or piece of wood measuring 1m (3¹/₃ft) in length. This is much easier than pulling out a tape measure each time.

TIP:
TIDY UP!
To keep your bunting tidy, organised and un-creased, store it wrapped around widths of cardboard. Write on the card how many metres or feet are on that length, so that when it comes to hanging it, you'll know where it goes.

ALTERNATIVE BUNTING IDEAS

Bunting is really versatile and you can adapt it in many ways to create something that will suit your day. Here are a few examples to inspire you.

Traditional pink bunting (above)

For this bunting I bought a bundle of pink fat quarters. These are great buys as the fabric colours and patterns are teamed together well. The traditional triangles were cut out using pinking shears and just sewn onto a long piece of ribbon using zigzag machine stitch.

Vintage petal bunting (above)

These fabrics were found in my mum's unused stash. They create a lovely vintage feel when teamed with a golden ribbon edged with lace. The petal shapes create a look that is softer than traditional bunting, providing a less fête-like style.

Doily bunting (above)

Using watercolour paints, I wetted these doilies and gently dabbed on the paint so that it bled across the paper to create a soft watercolour effect. I then cut them in half and attached them to a scrap piece of ribbon using a sewing machine. These could also be left white, folded in half and glued to garden string for a vintage outdoorsy look.

Double triangle bunting (above)

This is a playful adaptation of traditional bunting. By creating small triangles and mixing them in with large ones, you create a much softer, less dominant look. These were made without the need for sewing. Simply buy some fusible interfacing to glue the pennants to the ribbon. Use plain fabrics mixed with patterns and flowers to give a lovely sense of colour and texture.

Chunky bunting (below)

Square pennants with a pointy tip create yet another effect. This bunting was created from a fat quarter pack of fabrics. Be careful when sewing onto satin ribbon as I have here, as it can slip under the machine foot and create a wavy line. This bunting was created double-sided – I achieved this by using double-sided iron-on fusible interfacing to glue the two sides together.

Heart bunting (below)

This bunting is also no-sew. I used double-sided fusible interfacing to glue the fabric hearts together, making the entire thing double-sided. Try some customised appliqué embellishments as I have here. These were stuck on with the same fusible interfacing.

HOW I DID IT: TABLE COVERINGS

I did a lot of research into table coverings, and quickly discovered that it was very expensive to hire or buy them. I looked into several options, from using bedsheets or banquet rolls to disposable paper cloths. I then found out about sheeting fabric. Due to the extra-wide width of sheeting fabric, it is frequently used for making bed linen or for lining large quilts or drapery items. It is usually cheaper than most other fabrics and comes in different quality grades: the non-cotton variations are often wrinkle-free, which is perfect for table coverings. My local market sold 229cm (90in) sheeting which, when cut in half lengthways, was the perfect size to cover the lengths of my reception trestle tables.

The sheeting I bought was pure white, so I decided to add a splash of colour to each table with a runner. As well as being an extra decorative element, it can help to give the illusion of extra width to your tables. I used a pink gingham, which worked well with the blue gingham on the favour lids and the pink bows on the vases. I roughly laid this out at home on our dining table, using an old bedsheet and some flowers I had already created. I can't

advise doing this strongly enough – experimenting like this will really help your decision-making process.

To work out how much sheeting I needed, I visited my venue and laid out five trestle tables in a long row and placed a few chairs in position. This created one of the three full lengths of seating. From this I was able to calculate the right number of seats and I could check there was enough furniture of the correct size available. Once set up, I measured the table lengths and widths individually and together. I also set up the top table and food tables in the same way. From this I drew an exact plan of the room so I could always refer back to the number of tables and make any further calculations about other decorative items. It also helped to measure how far the fabric could drape off the sides and ends of the tables. From this visual plan I managed to work out how much sheeting and runner fabric I would need. I cut the sheeting into the correct widths and lengths using a pinking shear rotary cutter, which meant I didn't need to spend time hemming all the edges and the finish also echoed the bunting edges.

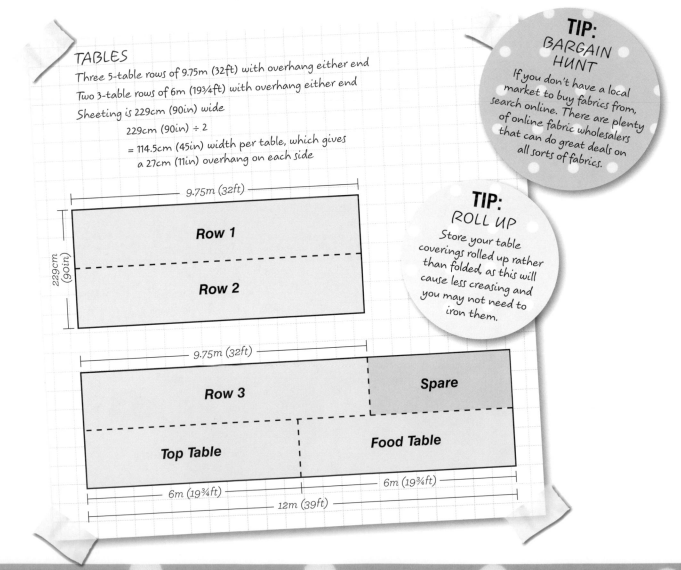

TABLES

Three 5-table rows of 9.75m (32ft) with overhang either end

Two 3-table rows of 6m (19¾ft) with overhang either end

Sheeting is 229cm (90in) wide

229cm (90in) ÷ 2

= 114.5cm (45in) width per table, which gives a 27cm (11in) overhang on each side

9.75m (32ft)

Row 1

229cm (90in)

Row 2

9.75m (32ft)

Row 3

Spare

Top Table

Food Table

6m (19¾ft)

6m (19¾ft)

12m (39ft)

TIP: BARGAIN HUNT
If you don't have a local market to buy fabrics from, search online. There are plenty of online fabric wholesalers that can do great deals on all sorts of fabrics.

TIP: ROLL UP
Store your table coverings rolled up rather than folded, as this will cause less creasing and you may not need to iron them.

TABLE DECORATIONS

When you start to think about your venue's décor, remember that the table decorations are probably the most important items to spend time on, as your guests will be sitting down at the table for long periods of time eating, drinking and listening to the speeches. If the small details are important to you, make sure you create them here.

You'll need to consider vases, flowers, candles, favours, place names, table numbers, cutlery, napkins and glasses, and possibly goody bags to entertain the children. Even if you need lots of these items, keep in mind not to overcrowd the tables. They will look messy and cramp your guests, so think about spreading out the decoration and limiting what you need.

I tried to save on table space by giving some of the items two jobs. For instance, some of the vases of flowers were quite tall so I also put the table numbers in the top. The cutlery was tied together with raffia with the place names attached. We didn't have candles, as the paper flowers would have presented a bit of a fire hazard, but we did have homemade candle favours for people to take home.

The table arrangement was tried and tested at home during the crafting process. By laying out a white bed sheet to the width of the tables and placing vases of different sizes along the sheet at different intervals, I was able to see what impact everything had, and to calculate the numbers I needed. At this stage I also placed a few of the other items on the mock-up table to see how it all fitted together and if it was too crowded. I kept the colours pink and blue to give a simple look to the table tops. I scribbled down the arrangement I was happy with so that I could remember it on set-up day.

Remember also that the top table is the main focus, so you might like to make this extra special with additional flowers, a decoupage 'Mr & Mrs' decoration, or even some photographs that mean something to both of you. If you're using a long table, you'll only have seating on one side, so you have a little more space to play with.

TABLE FLOWER PLAN

● Bourbon bottles
○ Short bottles
● Tall bottles

What I did...

Our trestle tables seated six people each and were organised in the room in three rows of five.

Each table had:
One tall bourbon bottle of flowers
Two smaller bottles of flowers
Six candle wedding favours
Six sets of wooden cutlery tied with place names
Six napkins
Two bottles of wine
Six wine glasses

Straight after our ceremony, guests were greeted at the reception with drinks and finger sandwiches in the garden. Once seated inside, we had the speeches followed by a buffet-style hog roast, so there was no need for plates on the tables – this was a huge space saver.

TIP:
KEEP IT CLEAR
Items such as favours could be placed elsewhere for people to take as they leave, or the cutlery could be collected by the guests at a buffet-style meal.

TIP:
CHAIR AWAY
If you're worried that space might be a little tight, consider the type of chairs you're using. High-backed, well-cushioned seating takes up a lot more space than simple country-style fold-up wooden chairs.

MAKE YOUR OWN FLOWERS

When I began, I thought I would only need around 300 stems to make all the table flowers. I originally chose seven different flower types, and made each in a different summer colour: orange lilies, red tulips, white daisies, pale pink peonies, yellow spidermums, deep pink dahlias and green carnations. I started with thirty of each variety, which gave me a total of 210 stems. I also tested out a variation of the daisy template to make a gerbera, which would make up the remaining numbers and also create the accessories. When I was nearing 300 stems I mocked up a table arrangement... and discovered that the amount I had made would barely be enough to decorate half the village hall: I needed double.

I burst into action, filling every spare moment with flower making to meet my target. I made the task easier by only making the flowers that were the fastest and easiest to make. Some of the flowers required me to draw out and cut individual petals, while others could be created on a large strip of paper, making the process much more time efficient. Gerberas are my favourite flower and naturally have a large surface area, meaning they have more impact on the tables and give the illusion of a fuller arrangement. They also happened to be the fastest to make, so these made up the extra 300 in the variety of colours that I had started with.

What you need

- Red crepe paper, 5.5 x 75cm (2¼ x 29½in) per flower (if you'd like the flower to appear bigger and fuller, make this strip longer)
- One length of paper-covered wire, 18 gauge
- Pinking shears
- Scissors
- Green floristry tape
- Ruler
- Pencil
- Red embroidery thread, 15cm (6in) per flower
- An old pillow (optional)

Instructions: carnation

1 Cut a strip of crepe paper 5.5 x 75cm (2¼ x 29½in); cut along one of the long sides with your pinking shears to create a zigzag edge. Gently stretch the pinked edge. Cut a 10–15cm (4–6in) strip of floristry tape and keep it nearby.

2 Gradually pinch and roll your paper strip around your wire with the pinked edge pointing up.

3 Pinching the paper and squeezing the bottom edge tightly as you go will help the top edge to splay out.

4 Securely tape your flower to the wire using your strip of floristry tape; wind the tape around the base of the flower. Once you are happy that the flower is secure, wrap the length of tape down the wire a little way to keep everything in place.

5 Cut a 15cm (6in) piece of embroidery thread and tie it around the base of your flower, approximately 1cm (½in) up from the bottom edge. Pull it tight and knot it in place; trim off the excess thread. This will open the flower out even further.

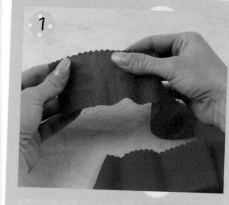
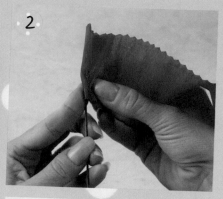

TIP: SAVE YOUR SWEATERS!

This tip applies to all the flowers on pages 87–95. Place an old pillow in your lap to rest the ends of the wires against when twisting and turning to attach the different flower elements. This will stop the wire from penetrating your clothing and causing lots of holes. I learnt the hard way!

What you need

- Yellow crepe paper, 8 x 20cm (3¼ x 8in) per flower centre
- White crepe paper, 50 x 30cm (20 x 12in)
- One length of paper-covered wire, 18 gauge
- Scissors
- Green floristry tape
- Ruler
- Pencil
- Templates from page 125
- An old pillow (optional)

Instructions: peony

1 To create the flower centre, cut a strip of yellow crepe paper 8 x 20cm (3¼ x 8in). Fold it in half lengthways and snip 3cm (1¼in) slits into the unfolded edge, about 2–3mm (⅛in) apart.

2 Firmly wrap the uncut folded edge around the top of your wire. Keep the bottom edge tight so that the cut ends splay outwards.

3 Attach the flower centre to the wire using a length of floristry tape. Wrap the tape tightly around the paper to secure it.

4 When the flower is secure, wrap the end of the tape down the wire a little way to fasten it off.

5 Using the peony templates on page 125, cut thirty large petals and ten small petals from white crepe paper, ensuring the paper grain runs up the length of your petals.

6 Using the thumb and forefinger of both hands, gently stretch each of the petals around the frilly edge and at the widest point.

TIP:
EASY PICK UP
Lay the cupped petals upside down on your work space, this makes them much easier to pick up when attaching.

7 Fold the base of each petal in half and twist 1cm (½in) up to create a cupped petal shape.

8 Start to position the small petals around the flower centre: the twists sit on top of the floristry tape.

9 Wind some tape around the base of the first round of petals to secure them, then continue to attach the rest of the petals in the same way; once you have finished attaching the small petals, move onto the large ones. Randomly overlap them slightly for a more natural look.

10 After each round of petals, wind the tape around to secure; hold the petals upwards with your fingers to keep them in shape and out of the way of the tape.

11 Keep checking the overall look of your petals as you add them, to ensure you create a pleasing arrangement.

What you need

- Yellow crepe paper, 12 x 10cm (4¾ x 4in) per flower centre, 16 x 20cm (6¼x 8in) for petals
- One length of paper-covered wire, 18 gauge
- Scissors
- Green floristry tape
- Ruler
- Pencil
- Template from page 124
- An old pillow (optional)

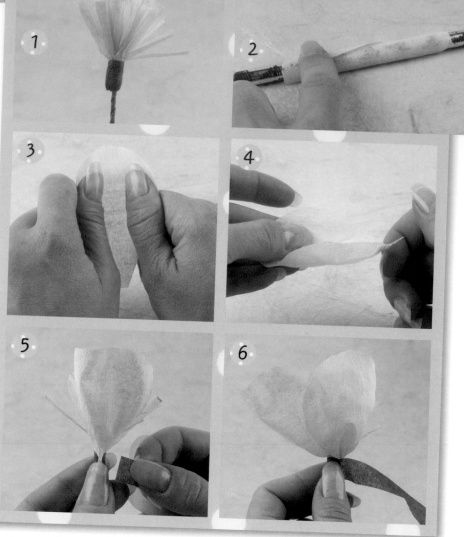

Instructions: tulip

1 Cut a 12 x 10cm (4¾ x 4in) rectangle of yellow crepe paper. Fold it in half lengthways and snip 4cm (1½in) long slits into the unfolded edge, approximately 2–3mm (1/8in) apart. Firmly wrap the uncut folded edge around the top of your wire and secure in place with floristry tape.

2 Use the tulip petal template (page 124) to cut eight petals from the yellow crepe, ensuring that the paper grain runs up the length of each petal. Roll each petal lengthways around a pencil, hold for a few seconds and release to create a cup shape.

3 Gently stretch the widest part of each petal between your thumbs and forefingers to create a fuller, more realistic shape. If you are gentle enough you can also stretch the very edge of the petal.

4 Tightly twist 1cm (½in) of the bottom edge of each petal.

5 Cut a small strip of tape and attach each petal one at a time, layering a petal with tape each time. Try to layer them so they overlap by half.

6 Continue until all the petals are attached and you are happy that they are all secure, then twist the excess tape down the wire to complete.

What you need

- Dark pink crepe paper, 17 x 24cm (6¾ x 9½in)
- One length of paper-covered wire, 18 gauge
- Scissors
- Green floristry tape
- Ruler
- Pencil
- Templates from page 125
- Three 7cm (2¾in) lengths of white DMC memory thread
- Two 7cm (2¾in) and one 10cm (4in) lengths of green DMC memory thread
- Hot glue gun (optional)
- An old pillow (optional)

Instructions: lily

1 Take each of your lengths of memory thread and fold one end back on itself by 5mm (¼in), then fold this at right angles to the rest of the length.

2 Wrap your six pieces of thread two at a time around the top of your paper-covered wire and tape them in place. If this is too fiddly, hot glue them.

3 Using the templates on page 125, create three large petals and three small ones. Make sure the grain of the paper runs up the length of the petals. Stretch the widest part of each petal between your thumbs and forefingers. This will make it naturally curve and appear fuller.

4 Wrap each petal around a pencil from the tip to just above the base, rolling into the natural curve you have just created. Hold for a few seconds and open it out. Let it relax a little.

5 Pinch a pleat at the base of each petal and twist to secure.

6 Cut a small length of tape and attach the three large petals, evenly spaced, around the top of the wire, attaching them so they curve outwards into a bloom. Twist any spare tape down the remaining length of the wire. Do the same with the three smaller petals, placing them in the gaps between the larger petals. Add a final layer of tape if you feel the petals need more security.

TIP:
CREATIVE COLOURING
You can try making the lily petals even more realistic by colouring the centre of each petal with a darker pink tone using pencil crayons. You could even try dotting on some spots with a felt tip pen.

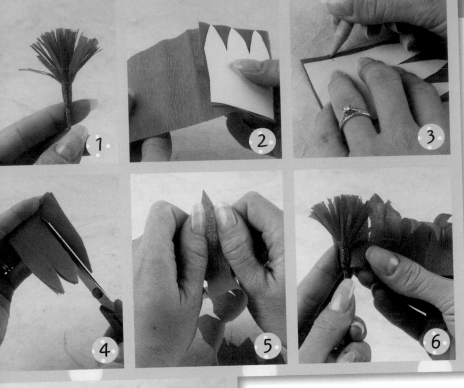

What you need

⊕ Orange crepe paper,
  8 x 12cm (3½ x 4¾in)
  per flower centre,
  19.5 x 30cm (7¾ x 12in) for
  the petals

⊕ One length of paper-
  covered wire, 18 gauge

⊕ Scissors

⊕ Green floristry tape

⊕ Ruler

⊕ Pencil

⊕ Templates from page 124

⊕ An old pillow (optional)

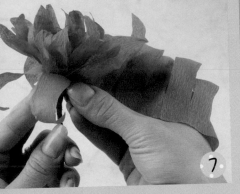

Instructions: dahlia

1 Cut a piece of orange crepe paper measuring 8 x 12cm (3½ x 4¾in). Fold it in half lengthways and snip 3cm (1¼in) long slits into the unfolded edge, approximately 2–3mm (⅛in) apart. Firmly wrap the uncut folded edge around the top of your wire and secure in place with floristry tape.

2 Cut three 30cm (12in) lengths of crepe paper: they should correspond to the heights of the three templates, so make one 5cm (2in) tall, one 6.5cm (2½in) tall and one 8cm (3¼in) tall. Fold each length of crepe into a concertina the width of the corresponding template.

3 Draw around each of your templates onto the folded crepe paper and mark the horizontal trim line on each edge as a guide.

4 Cut out the petal shapes, then snip down between the petals as far as your marked line. Open out the concertina and cut down the fold lines as far as your marked line to create one continuous strip of petals.

5 Very carefully stretch the end of each individual petal on all three strips of paper, using your thumbs and forefingers.

6 Roll the ends of the petals around a pencil, rolling into the curve created in step 5. This is easiest to do on the edge of a table, as you can position your hand underneath to start the petals rolling around the pencil. Hold for a few seconds and release. Starting with the smallest strip of petals, wrap and pinch the paper around your flower centre so that the petals curve inwards, then tape securely into place.

7 Attach the medium strip of petals in the same way, with the petals curving inwards. On the largest strip, attach the paper to the flower centre so that the petals curve outwards. Secure the entire flower with an extra strip of tape, and work this down the wire to finish for extra security.

What you need

- ⊛ White crepe paper, 10 x 12cm (4 x 4¾in) per flower centre
- ⊛ Pale pink crepe paper, 60 x 16cm (24 x 4½in)
- ⊛ One length of paper-covered wire, 18 gauge
- ⊛ Long scissors
- ⊛ Green floristry tape
- ⊛ Ruler
- ⊛ Pencil
- ⊛ An old pillow (optional)

Instructions: spidermum

1 Cut a piece of white crepe paper measuring 10 x 12cm (4 x 4¾in). Fold it in half lengthways and snip 4cm (1½in) slits into the folded edge, approximately 2–3mm (⅛in) apart. Firmly wrap the unfolded edge around the top of your wire and secure in place with floristry tape.

2 Cut a 60cm (24in) length of pink crepe paper that tapers from 16cm (6½in) wide at one end to 8cm (3¼in) wide at the other. Do this by marking out each 30cm (12in) point along the length. Starting at the tallest point mark 16cm (6½in) – then 30cm (12in) along the length mark a height of 12cm (4½in) and then 8cm (3¼in) at the end. Connect these height markers together with your pencil and ruler and cut it out.

3 Gently fold the strip in half, lengthways. Along the open edge of the piece, mark a guideline 1.5cm (⅔in) from the edge, up the whole length.

4 Snip slits into the folded edge as far as your guideline, spacing the slits about 2–3mm (⅛in) apart; you will need long scissors for the wider end.

5 Starting at the shorter end, wrap the length of petals onto the wire, pinching it roughly as you go to separate the petals and stop them lying directly on top of one another.

6 Once you reach the end, attach the petals with a length of tape, cutting enough to wind plenty down the wire for extra security.

ALTERNATIVE PAPER FLOWER IDEAS

If you'd like to create flowers that are more abstract in nature and far quicker and easier to make than those shown on pages 86–93, then these examples could be for you. They all have impact on their own and you can change the colours and patterns to suit your wedding style.

Cupcake flowers (below)

Fold four cupcake cases into eighths and cut a semi-circle into the fluted edge. Open all four out and push a wire through the middle; attach each layer individually with hot glue to separate the petals.

These can be easily adapted by adding embellishments such as buttons to the flower centre. You can also experiment, as I have below, with cutting different shapes into the fluted edge, using different numbers of cases or layering different size cases together to give different effects.

Tissue paper circle flower (below)

These are really easy! Use between ten and twenty pre-cut tissue paper circles layered together and fastened in the centre with wire or staples. Pull each layer upwards, pinching at the base to create a simple fluffy flower.

Magazine flowers (right)

Use up old magazines or newspapers by making these. Fold a magazine page in half along the long edge and then fold those edges back to the centre line to create a concertina. Snip at regular intervals along the folded edges and attach to a wire or wooden skewer by wrapping the petals around and up slightly to give a fuller flower. Secure with masking tape and then cover with floral tape.

Swirly rose (below)

Make a 7.5 x 7.5cm (3 x 3in), 15 x 15cm (6 x 6in), or 20.5 x 20.5cm (8 x 8in) diameter spiral out of card. Curl up the spiral from the outer edge to the inside. Allow to loosen slightly and then hot glue gun together. You can experiment with different effects by cutting a wavy line or changing the sizes of your spirals. The larger they are the fuller they look.

MAKE YOUR OWN VASES

Recycling bottles and jars to make vases is really easy, effective and on-trend. I created two types of vase. The first put Dave's ten-year collection of bourbon bottles to good use as the centrepiece for each table; each had a very simple, pink raffia bow tied around the neck. The second type of vase was wrapped with yarn. Ask friends and family to collect up old bottles and jars, and consider decorating them with lace, fabric, glitter – or anything else that works with your theme.

What you need

⊕ Bottle or jar
⊕ Your choice of yarn: I used white 2-ply (lace-weight)
⊕ Double-sided tape
⊕ Hot glue gun (optional)

Instructions: yarn-wrapped vases

1 Stick double-sided tape firmly around the very top and bottom of your bottle and then position four evenly spaced vertical strips down the sides. Take care not to overlap the tape, but get very close.

2 Peel off the non-sticky layer of the tape from around the neck of the bottle. Make a 90 degree angle with your yarn and hold it in place so the cut end points towards the bottom of the bottle.

3 Start to wrap the yarn tightly around the neck of the bottle so that it secures the loose end in place. Make sure that the yarn doesn't overlap in the rotations but is close enough that there are no gaps.

4 Continue wrapping the bottle until you reach the bottom; gradually peel down the non-sticky layer of the tape on the sides as you go. When you have finished wrapping, cut the yarn end and add a blob of hot glue to it to hold it in place. Be careful not to allow the glue to drip to the bottom, otherwise the bottle will not stand flat.

TIP:
YARN TIME
If you want results fast, use a thicker yarn that will cover the vase quickly and give a chunkier appearance.

What you need

⊕ Bottle or jar

⊕ 90cm (35½in) fuchsia raffia
– you may want to try this out
and then adjust it, depending
on the size of your bottle

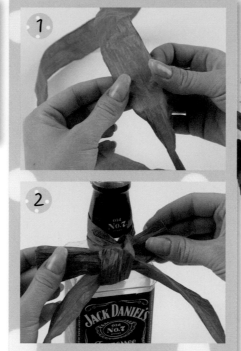

Instructions:
vases with pink raffia bows

1 Cut your length of raffia and
gently open it out into a flat piece
of ribbon.

2 Tie it around the neck of your
bottle, as you would tie a shoelace,
taking extra care to try to keep the
ribbon flat and uncrumpled. Don't
pull it too tight or it may rip.

3 Cut your ribbon ends to the
same length and at angles
opposite to each other.

What you need

⊕ Vase

⊕ Your choice of handmade flowers:
I used thirteen in different colours
and varieties

⊕ Salt

TIP:
SUPER SALT
I used salt as a bottle filler
because it was much cheaper
and more readily available than
other floristry vase fillers, plus
it hides the green wire stems.
To get the most for your
money, buy it from a
wholesaler.

ALTERNATIVE VASE IDEAS
Once you have mastered the yarn-
wrapping technique, use different yarns
or even garden twine to create different
effects and styles.

Instructions: arranging handmade flowers

1 Fill your bottles with salt.

2 Push the stems of your chosen flowers into the salt. At this stage, start to
bend the necks of the wire flowers slightly so the blooms don't all sit on top
of one another. Space them out in an arrangement that you like. You may
need to trim off some excess wire at the bottom to suit your arrangement.

DECORATING THE TOP TABLE

The top table is commonly a long table facing the room of guests, so that when the speeches are happening people can look on. The seating often follows a traditional layout, with the bride and groom sitting together in the middle of the table. Next to the bride are the bride's father, then the groom's mother, followed by the best man. Next to the groom would be the bride's mother, then the groom's father, followed by the maid of honour. However, many people these days opt for a round top table, or sit with their bridesmaids and groomsmen if parents on either side are separated: don't feel that you have to stick to a layout if it doesn't work for you and your families.

If, like us, you have limited space for the top table, or just don't want to do everything the traditional way, you could sit the best man and maid of honour in amongst the the rest of your guests – close enough to remain important but with their own families. In a further break with tradition, we sat our parents next to each other as we knew they would be more comfortable with this arrangement.

I didn't have any big plans for the top table decoration. I didn't want it to be too over-styled as it wouldn't have suited our country-style wedding, and I wanted it to remain in keeping with all the other tables. I added the same elements to it as the guest tables, but with a few extra personalisations. The bourbon flower arrangement bottles represented the bride and groom. In front of Dave was the traditional, iconic black label and in front of me was a honey bourbon bottle, with a cream-coloured label, which reflected my dress and my preferred flavour. These also reflected my bride and groom mini wedding cake topper bottles.

Since both sets of our parents are still happily married, we placed photographs on the wall behind us of them on their wedding days. This helped to make the area surrounding us personal and showed our respect and thanks to them for being such good role models.

Running along the front of the table I placed MR & MRS cardboard blanks that I had decorated with colourful decoupage paper. These helped to highlight the top table as well as emphasise our marriage. This was a sudden decision, made simply because I walked into my local craft store to find the blanks on offer! They were really easy to make, but did take nearly a whole day (see right for some guidance and ideas).

TIP:
SPATIAL AWARENESS
When planning your room's layout, remember to give yourself enough space to get in and out of your seat, especially if you have a large dress. Also, if you plan on handing out any gifts, such as flowers to thank people for their help, you may need to keep them behind the top table to be easily accessible, so consider this when planning.

Decorating decoupage letters

Step 1 Gather together papers that match your colour scheme and rip them into small pieces. I used free patterned paper inserts from card-making magazines.

Step 2 Paint small areas of the cardboard with PVA glue and stick the pieces of paper onto it in a random pattern. Overlap the paper pieces and fold them around the sides of the letters. As you start to build up your layers, paint PVA glue over the top of all layers to seal them.

Step 3 Continue in this way until each letter is covered. Be careful not to let the letters get stuck to anything while they are drying. I found that, if I started at the top of the letter, by the time I got to the bottom it was dry enough at the top to stand and not get stuck to any surfaces.

TIP:
SNAP HAPPY
Personalise your MR & MRS letters by printing out lots of your favourite photographs of each other and tearing them into small pieces in such a way that your faces are still visible. Collage them onto the letters for a really personal look.

FAVOURS

Traditionally favours are given to wedding guests as a token of thanks for sharing in your special day. Sugared almonds, chocolates and other candies are popular gifts, although it's common these days to think outside the box and give items such as a lottery ticket or a charity pin badge to each guest. Bear in mind your guestlist when you start thinking about what favours you want: creating handcrafted items might seem like a wonderful idea, but consider how many items you will need to make, and how much time it will take. Also, work out a careful budget, as the cost of even relatively cheap items quickly adds up when you buy or make a large number.

For our wedding I wanted to achieve something on a low budget. I wanted to make favours that were unusual, and which could be made far in advance and stored ready for the day. I really liked the idea of homemade truffles or cookies, but these would need to be made in the few days leading up to the wedding, which I felt I wouldn't have time for. So I decided on candles.

Although there are plenty of complicated methods for making candles, I found a candle-making method that was really simple, using soy wax as a base and dye flakes to add colour. I felt this was manageable, so I started to think about how I could present my candles. Many high-end supermarket desserts are now available to buy in solid glass ramekins, which are so nice that you feel you shouldn't just recycle them... Instead, if you're anything like me, you'll store them up in your cupboard and never get round to using them! I had four lurking in a cupboard, and I decided there must be other people out there who had done the same. I went onto my social network page and onto a local wedding social media page, and put out a request for spare glass ramekins. Within a few days I had several messages and over 150 jars. They were free of charge and perfect for my candle favours.

TIP: CUTTING COSTS
Not only were the jars free of charge, I researched the materials needed for the candles online and found the cheapest option. I also found a double boiler being given away for free online.

For the kids

Votive candles were ideal favours for the adults, but not for the children. I was a bit concerned about the children throughout the speeches. I was worried they might get bored and start making a commotion if not entertained. I decided to design party bags full of toys and colouring books to keep them happy. Each child had one on their seat ready for when they sat down.

LIBBY'S PARTY BAG

MAKE YOUR OWN CANDLES

Even though I used a very simple candle-making method, it is still far easier if you can find a friend or family member to help you. I had my mother-in-law to help me as she had candle-making experience. I am going to show you how to make 100 votive candles in glass ramekins; if you are using different-sized containers, please see right for guidance on how to calculate your wax, dye and fragrance quantities.

Candle-making maths...

Here's how to calculate wax, dye and fragrance quantities for your own votive candles.

Per 100g (⅓oz) wax you will need:

1g (¹⁄₃₀₀oz) dye flakes
5ml (⅕ fl oz) fragrance oil

To work out your quantity of wax, place your glass container on a set of scales and set the display to zero. Fill your container with water. Take your water weight in ounces and multiply it by 0.86. Convert your answer to grams. I cheated and did this online.

My calculations are below:
Water weight = 4oz
4 x 0.86 = 3.44oz
3.44oz = 97.522g wax per glass container
So for 100 containers: 97.522g x 100 = 9,752.2 grams, rounded up to 10kg (22lb) wax

What you need

For 100 candles made in glass ramekins:

- ✪ 10kg (22lb) soy wax flakes
- ✪ 100g (¼lb) turquoise dye flakes
- ✪ 110 natural pre-waxed votive wicks
- ✪ 500ml (16.9fl oz) sweet pea fragrance oil
- ✪ 100 glass ramekins
- ✪ Double boiler or glass bowl over a saucepan of boiling water
- ✪ Metal ladle
- ✪ Old wooden spoon
- ✪ Pourable measuring jug
- ✪ Mini measuring glass
- ✪ Lots of pencils or chop sticks
- ✪ Apron
- ✪ Gloves (optional)

For 100 lids:

- ✪ 2.5m (8¼ft) of blue gingham fabric
- ✪ 90m (295¼ft) pink raffia cut into 90cm (35½in) lengths
- ✪ Pencil
- ✪ Plate measuring 15cm (6in) in diameter
- ✪ Pinking shears
- ✪ 100 small elastic bands
- ✪ Paper tags (optional: for place names or thank you notes)

Instructions: making the candles

1 Lay out your glass ramekins in rows, with one or two wicks in the centre of each, propped up with a pencil or chop stick.

2 Place your double boiler (or glass bowl over a saucepan) on the cooker top. Pour hot water into the bottom boiler and keep it hot, not boiling. Measure out 1kg (35¼oz) of soy wax flakes and pour them into your top boiler pan; keep them moving with a wooden spoon.

3 Keep the flakes moving until they completely melt and become transparent.

4 Measure out 10g (⅓oz) of dye flakes and add to the wax. Stir until the flakes melt.

5 Measure out 50ml (1¾fl oz) of fragrance oil; add to the wax and stir in.

SAFETY FIRST

Only use very gentle heat and, once the wax is melted, turn off the stove and take it away from the heat. Candle wax melts below the boiling point of water. This is why using a double boiler, or heatproof bowl over a smaller saucepan of water is advisable, to help stop the wax overheating. Candle wax should not reach above 90°C (194°F). Use a cooking thermometer, if you have one, but if your wax starts to smoke, or vaporise, it is too hot and could catch fire. If this happens, turn off your stove and cover the pan with a lid or damp cloth. You must never pour water onto a wax fire.

6 Once the flakes have completely melted, turn off your stove and move the double boiler away from the heat. Ladle the liquid wax into your measuring jug. Gently pour the wax into your glass containers to the desired level, keeping the wicks upright as you do so. This is where a second pair of hands is really useful! Take care as you come towards the end of your melted wax – it is important not to leave any jars half-filled, as pouring fresh melted wax on top of set wax can cause it to bubble and can look unsightly. If you have a little melted wax left, simply return it to the double boiler and just melt the next batch on top.

7 Place your double boiler back on to the heat and repeat steps 1–6 until all your jars are filled.

8 Leave the candles to harden slightly before moving them elsewhere to properly set overnight. After 24 hours, once the wax has hardened, cut your wicks down to the desired length. You may need to bend them in order to fit your lid.

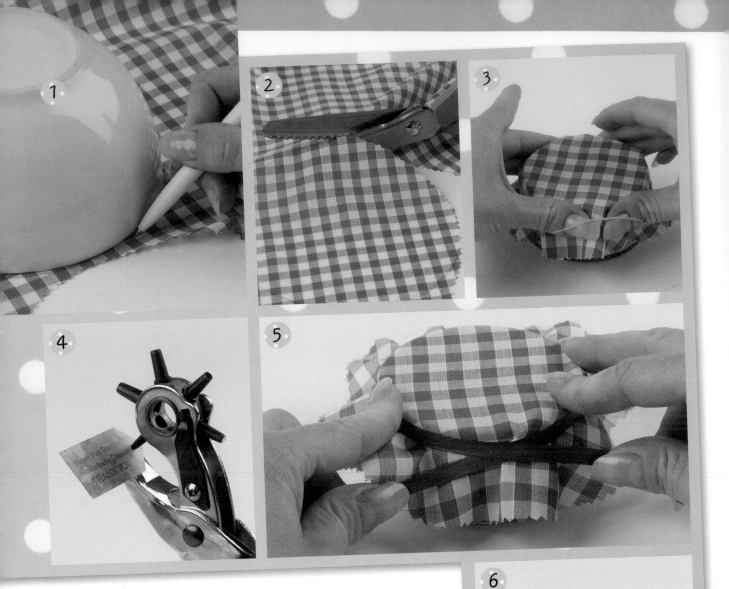

Instructions: making the lids

1 Find a plate or other circular item measuring 15cm (6in) in diameter that is suitable to draw around. Place it on your blue gingham fabric and draw one circle for each candle. Make sure they are close together to get the most out of your fabric with minimal waste.

2 Cut out your circles using pinking shears.

3 Place a gingham circle centrally on top of a candle, bending the wick if necessary. Secure it with an elastic band around the rim.

4 Prepare your tags, if necessary, by punching a hole in each. See page 111 for ideas for how to create a tag.

5 Take one of your 90cm (35½in) lengths of raffia. Fold it in half and wrap both sides towards you around the rim.

6 Cross the raffia over and add your tag, then wrap the raffia back to the start and tie it securely with a knot. You may need an extra pair of hands to hold everything in place while you tie it off.

TIP:
KEEP A LID ON IT
You may want to experiment with different lid sizes, depending on the size of your jar...

7 Open out the ends of the raffia and carefully tie a neat bow, being careful not to crumple it too much or tear it as you pull it through. Neatly cut the ends at opposite angles to each other.

TIP:
VERSATILE VOTIVES
You could tie a small tag to your raffia bow detailing what's inside, or you could make the candle as your place name. See details on how to make this on page 111.

MAKE YOUR OWN LANTERNS

Outdoor lanterns are one of those elements that can bring a fantastic atmosphere to an outside space. They can serve a purpose if it is particularly dark outside, to illuminate pathways or outdoor areas, but I made them for pure visual indulgence. They need patience and a cool day to make as they do take time. I gave this job to my dad, as he is handy with a hammer.

What you need

⊗ Tin cans

⊗ Template from page 127

⊗ Hammer

⊗ Strong nail or a bradawl

⊗ White spray paint suitable for metal

⊗ Paper and cardboard

⊗ Turn table

⊗ Tea lights

⊗ To support the can during hammering, I used a 7.5 x 7.5cm (3 x 3in) piece of timber with a 'V'-shaped notch cut into it. Alternatively, you could use wooden blocks or bricks instead

Instructions

1 Thoroughly wash out the cans and remove the labels. Fill the cans almost to the top with water and stand them up in the freezer for a couple of hours, until the water is solid. Be careful not to freeze them for too long, or they could split.

2 For each lantern you want to make, copy and cut a template (see page 127), and cut another piece of blank paper to the same size. Wrap the blank paper around your frozen can, place the template on top, and secure them in place with masking tape. Do this one can at a time, to prevent the ice melting while you work. The layer of blank paper will give your template some extra support as the ice starts to melt.

The supporting block I used.

TIP:
COPYCAT
Rather than trying to re-use the same template, take several photocopies and use a fresh one for each can. Otherwise you will eventually lose sight of where the dots are for hammering.

3 Place the can on a hard surface with supports on either side. With your bradawl or nail and hammer, quickly pierce a hole through each dot on your template.

4 Remove the template and allow the tin to dry.

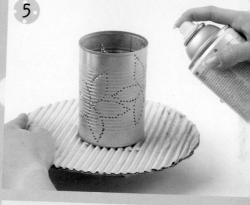

5 Place some cardboard on top of your turn table and stand the can on top. Gently spray an even layer of paint onto the outside of the can, turning the table as you go. Try not to clog up the holes.

6 Once dry, pop a tea light candle inside for a stylish glowing lantern.

TIP: SUPPORT IT!
Don't simply hammer the can on a flat surface, as this will cause it to bend and flatten as the ice starts to melt.

TIP: MAKE IT YOUR OWN
You could design your own template for any size of can by measuring the circumference and height. Draw a rectangle from those measurements and cut it out to check for size. Draw your design onto the rectangle and spread some dots about on your lines ready for piercing. Remember to photocopy your template to use again.

TIP: HANG UPS
If you would prefer to hang your lanterns, pierce a hole near the top of the can on either side. Use a sturdy piece of wire as a hanger. Some of your scrap floristry wire would be ideal for this.

ALTERNATIVE LANTERN IDEAS

If you want lanterns that require less effort, why not save a selection of jars and decorate them with lace, string, ribbons and buttons? Here I created a vintage theme, but you could easily add colour to suit your style.

CHALKBOARD

To keep things ticking along smoothly on the day, I made a chalkboard detailing the timings of the main events. As it was a very relaxed wedding, we didn't have a master of ceremonies to keep everything and everyone moving along, and this seemed like the perfect alternative.

To make my chalkboard, I bought a piece of MDF board, 91.5 x 61cm (36 x 24in) in size and 6mm (¼in) thick – sturdy enough to stand up on its own. I painted it with three coats of chalkboard paint; thick black masonry paint would probably work just as well.

I initially researched other people's chalkboard designs online, and downloaded some free fonts that looked a little like the font used on the bourbon bottle labels, as I wanted the different elements of the day to link together. I created my design on screen at the correct size using Adobe InDesign.

MR & MRS MIALL'S WEDDING DAY CELEBRATIONS

FRIDAY AUGUST 2nd 2013

3pm - Ceremony
3:45pm - Photos
4:30pm- Reception drinks
6pm - Speeches
6:30pm - Pig Roast
8pm - Evening guests arrive
9pm - Cake cutting

TIP:
SCALE IT UP
If you don't have the facilities to design onscreen, draw something to scale and enlarge it on a photocopier over several pages that you can then stick together. Otherwise, stick lots of sheets of paper together to the size of your board and draw the design full-size.

TIP:
MAKE IT STICK
Liquid chalk is better for a display that will be moved around and could get bumped, as it won't smudge or rub away except with a damp cloth.

I printed my design full-size by tiling it onto several pieces of paper and then accurately cutting and pasting it all together. Next, I rubbed a thick layer of chalk all over the back of the design and carefully stuck it on top of my painted board. Using a blunt coloured pencil (a sharp one would make it harder to see the line and potentially rip the paper) I accurately traced the outlines of my design firmly on top of my print-out. I took care not to rub the side of my hand on the board as I only wanted a chalky outline of the text to appear when I took the paper away.

Once I had traced everything through, I removed the print-out and used a liquid chalk pen to go over the chalk outline and fill in the white lettering. I used a ruler to get straight edges for the outside borders.

When I had finished and the liquid chalk had dried, I rubbed away the excess chalk with an old dry cloth to reveal my cleanly written chalkboard.

SIGNAGE

You may not have a need for signs like this on your big day. For me, they were an added extra simply because I had the use of a computer and the skills to make them up fairly quickly. Because we had a candy and cake stall, I wanted to create labels and note cards telling people what was on display. Again, I did a little bit of research to try and find a traditional candy jar label template. I found a shape that I was able to re-create and designed it in a similar style to all the other stationery, using scanned fabrics and colours seen throughout the wedding (see page 125 for a template).

For each of the cakes, I made a smaller version of the candy label and placed it close to each item. I even made a notice for the main wedding cake as I was concerned people might start tucking into it too early! I also created some labels for the card table, and some arrows directing the guests to the bathrooms and cloakroom.

SEATING PLAN

A seating plan is a must: it will help the day run smoothly by ensuring that your guests all know where to sit. It is one of the last jobs to do before the day, as you can almost guarantee that a few guests will drop out at short notice. It can be quite stressful ensuring that everyone is sitting with someone they know, but try not to get too anxious about it, as there's no right or wrong way to arrange people, and they will be free to move around after the speeches anyway.

There are so many creative ways to display a seating plan: a quick search online will bring up a multitude of ideas, from window panes and folding screens, to vintage suitcases, maps, corkboards and over-size picture frames. Regardless of the theme of your wedding, and how much time and effort you want to spend on it, it should be relatively easy to choose a display that fits. Some venues will include the use of an easel, or similar, so ask to see this before the day.

I wanted our table plan to be a visual key that was easy to decipher. The tables were very long so I felt we needed to show exactly where people were seated so that guests weren't wandering up and down the room trying to find their name. To do this I drew up the rough dimensions of the room, adding in doors and all the furniture. I wrote the guest names on the table spaces and then had an alphabetical key underneath with a table number for each person.

I decided to have two table plans on display, one at either end of the room. Both were printed to A2 size (about 16½ x 23½in) by tiling the pieces together and cutting and pasting carefully in line. I then pasted them onto mountboard and displayed them on an artist's easel.

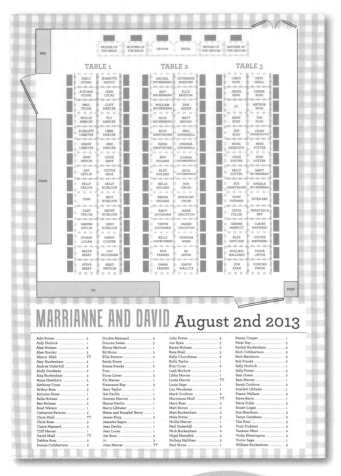

MARRIANNE AND DAVID August 2nd 2013

TIP:
PLAN B

You could make your table plan really simple by listing your guest names on decorative pieces of card headed with the table numbers. These could then be attached to a larger board to be displayed in your reception room. This works really well, so long as the table numbers are easy to spot within the room. If you wanted to be more creative you could display the cards on the board in the same layout as the tables themselves.

Labelling the tables

Whether you number, name or assign each table with an image or photograph, it's important to make them distinct. I chose a simple numbering system. The table numbers were made in a similar style to the other signage on page 109. I designed them as circles that were cut out and stuck back to back onto wires that were pushed into the taller flower arrangements on each table.

PLACE NAMES

There are many ways you can display place names, from writing names on clothes pegs and clipping them to wine glass stems, to attaching the guest's name to the stick of an upturned cake pop, or even spelling names out with Scrabble™ tiles! Simply choose an idea that works with your theme. If this sounds a little time-consuming and/or expensive, one of the simplest options is to use a folded piece of card, with the guest's name written on one side. You could keep them very simple or make them decorative, perhaps with a die-cut design. But of course, the most important thing is simply that people know where to sit!

For our wedding I decided to incorporate the place names in a way that reduced clutter on the tables: I made mini luggage tags and tied them with raffia to the wooden cutlery. This helped to keep the cutlery neat and ensured that every guest had some. I still kept the overall design theme running through the place names. I did this by re-using some of the elements, such as the scanned gingham fabric and the fonts.

The luggage tags were double-sided. One side was kept very simple with the scanned blue gingham fabric that had been used in the invitations. This mirrored the bunting as well as the lids for the candle favours. Guest names were typed on the reverse on top of an image I had found of sweet pea flowers – this reflected the candle scent. Keeping the styling simple in this way meant that the colours on the tables remained minimal, helping to create the illusion of space.

Making mini luggage tags

Step 1 Scan the template provided on page 126. Drop it into your computer programme and copy and paste it several times to fill the page, butting the lines up against each other; you can squeeze several onto an A4 (8¼ x 11¾in) sheet.

Step 2 Type the text you want onto each tag, altering the font or text colour to match your theme or, if you want to hand-write them, leave blank. Apply a coloured or image background if you want, remembering that the background needs to be light enough that you can still read the text.

Step 3 Once you have printed and cut out your designs, embellish them with ribbon, lace, buttons or even diamantés to link them with your theme, if appropriate. There are many opportunities here to be really creative.

These tags for our candle favours were made in exactly the same way, except they had a note of thanks on, rather than a name.

THE CAKE

I made our wedding cake which, to save on cost, was also the dessert course of our wedding breakfast. It took me most of the week before the wedding to make and decorate, so if you want a homemade cake but can't get enough time off work, consider baking the cake in advance and freezing it, or else delegate this job to someone else.

Having made a two-tier cake for Dave's 30th birthday a few years previously, I knew what recipe I wanted to use and I was familiar with the process of dowelling a cake to support the layers. For our wedding cake, I wanted to introduce a third tier.

I made the top and bottom tiers from madeira cake. As it has a dense consistency and is therefore quite heavy, I was concerned that having madeira for the middle tier as well might cause the bottom tier to collapse under the weight. So instead, I made a rich chocolate cake for the middle tier. I cut all the cakes in half and filled them: I used chocolate buttercream for the madeira cakes and a vanilla buttercream for the chocolate cake. This helped keep the layers moist and gave the cake a stripy effect when cut.

As it had been a while since I last baked the recipes, and I was using a different oven, I decided to do a test run of both cakes. I also iced both and practised different types of decoration.

I found some visual inspiration online for the decoration, as at first I wasn't sure what I wanted. I decided on a fairly simple cake covered in bold and beautiful sugar gerberas in the same colours as the table flowers; I also researched three-dimensional sugar flowers for the top of the cake. I found online tutorials to show me how to make them – it was tricky, but I managed it.

TIP:
WEIGHTY MATTERS

Research online and consider contacting a professional cake maker to assess the size and weight of your proposed tiers. Some types of cake are much denser than others, and if you position the heavier cakes at the top, you may risk the whole cake collapsing in on itself.

TIP:
TRIAL RUN

Try and find time for a test run, as you are likely to learn a lot from this. I discovered that I had problems getting an even bake in our powerful oven. Because I'd given myself enough time, I managed to find a really good trick to prevent this. Soaking strips of old towel in water and pinning them to the outside of the tin during baking stopped the outer edge cooking too quickly and helped the cake to bake more evenly.

Transporting the cake

I made our cake in the week leading up to the wedding. It was huge: the bottom layer alone was 35.5cm (14in) in diameter. When baked I named it 'Monster Cake'! To be able to decorate the full three tiers of cake, I had to place it on a cake stand as it was so heavy it wouldn't slide around on the work surface. Having it on a stand meant I could get my hands underneath to rotate it. The cake was stored in my kitchen for the duration of the process, usually covered with a tea towel. I decided not to buy a cake box to transport it, as they are really expensive and I knew I wouldn't use it again. We ended up fashioning a cake-carrying box from an old, fully sterilised dog basket, as this was the only container large enough. We screwed some wooden batons into the base, so that we were able to get our fingers underneath it to lift it out, and then placed a non-slip mat in the bottom, to prevent it sliding. In the end, shifting the cake around proved quite a task.

Other people I know, who have made their own 'naked' wedding cakes – less formal cakes without a layer of fondant (sugarpaste) on top – were able to take the cake to the venue on the morning of the wedding in pieces and assemble it there. The layers were held together with lemon mascarpone cream, and then the whole cake was decorated very simply with wedding toppers, fresh fruit and flowers and a dusting of icing sugar. If you don't like the thought of transporting the cake after assembling it, check with your venue whether this option is feasible. Assembling the cake at the venue requires less in the way of preparation, but I would strongly advise you to have a trial run, so that you uncover any pitfalls in advance and can quickly achieve exactly what you want.

Cake toppers

I found inspiration for our cake toppers in our drinks cupboard! I put two mini bourbon bottles together and we had a bride and groom. A turquoise blue tie and handkerchief as well as a white gerbera buttonhole/boutonniere adorned one mini bottle. The cream-coloured mini bourbon bottle mimicked my dress colour, so I glued some diamantés along the top of the label, and made a mini veil for the bottle top.

DECORATE YOUR CAKE

If you would like to decorate your cake in the same style that I did, using gerberas, or indeed any other flower, this is how to achieve it. You'll need to bake your cakes following your favourite recipe and leave them to cool before attempting these instructions.

What you need

To stack the cakes:

- ✪ Your choice of cakes
- ✪ Hardboard cake boards the same size as the base of each cake tier
- ✪ Fondant (sugarpaste) to cover each cake and board
- ✪ 6mm (¼in) food-safe dowels
- ✪ Mitre saw or heavy duty scissors and knife
- ✪ Cocktail stick
- ✪ Buttercream

For the iced decorations:

- ✪ Cake modelling ball tool
- ✪ Foam flower-making pad
- ✪ Plastic or polystyrene flower former cups
- ✪ Three gerbera plunge cutters: 45mm, 56mm and 70mm (1¾in, 2¼in and 2¾in)
- ✪ Non-stick icing sheet
- ✪ 15mm (²⁄₃in) circle cutter
- ✪ Small brush
- ✪ Edible glue
- ✪ 25g (⁴⁄₅oz) gum tragacanth powder
- ✪ 250g (8¾oz) ready-made fondant (sugarpaste) in black, red, orange, yellow, white, pale pink and fuchsia
- ✪ Icing (powdered) sugar
- ✪ Small pair of sharp scissors
- ✪ Palette knife

Instructions: stacking your cakes

1 Ice the cakes and their corresponding boards with white fondant (sugarpaste), ensuring a smooth, even coverage. Measure the centre point of your bottom tier of cake and mark it with a cocktail stick.

2 Deduct 1.25cm (½in) from the radius of your second cake tier; mark four evenly spaced points at this distance from your central mark.

3 Keeping it as vertical as possible, insert one of your lengths of dowel into the cake at your central mark.

4 Mark the dowel with a pencil at the height of the cake.

5 Remove the dowel and cut it at your pencil line – you can use a mitre saw to do this or score it with a knife and use heavy duty scissors to cut the rest of the way through. Cut four more pieces of dowel the same length. Push all your pieces of dowel into place. If you are making a cake with three or more tiers, as I did on the day (see left), you will need to insert lengths of dowel into all the tiers except the top tier before you start to stack them. In this example I have used two tiers.

6 Spread a thin layer of buttercream onto the second tier cake board and secure your second cake tier onto it. Then apply a thin layer of buttercream over the top of the dowels and stack your second tier in place. I find this helps it to stick and is extra security when transporting the cake.

7 Repeat step 6 to attach any further tiers. To hide the joins between your layers, lightly dust your work surface with icing (powdered) sugar and roll out some white fondant (sugarpaste) 2–3mm (about ⅛in) thick. Use your 15mm (⅔in) circle cutter to cut several circles. Using icing (powdered) sugar to coat your hands, gently roll the circles into small balls. Using the cutter ensures the balls will all be the same size. Keep going until you have enough balls to surround and conceal each cake board.

8 Stick these fondant (sugarpaste) balls around the joins of your cake tiers, using your brush to paint on a little edible glue first to hold them in place.

TIP: STRAIGHTEN UP
It is very important that your dowels are inserted into your cakes absolutely vertically, otherwise they will not support the weight of your tiers. They must all be exactly the same length, otherwise your cakes won't be level.

Instructions: flat flowers

1 To strengthen the fondant (sugarpaste) and make it fit for modelling you will need to add gum tragacanth to it. For each 250g (8¾oz) of fondant (sugarpaste), add 1tsp of gum tragacanth and knead until fully mixed. Wrap up well and place in an airtight container overnight.

2 Lightly dust your work surface with icing (powdered) sugar and roll out your choice of fondant (sugarpaste) to approximately 2mm (¹⁄₈in) thick.

3 Use the 70mm (2¾in) gerbera plunge cutter to cut the gerbera shape and then depress the plunge to indent the petal pattern. Repeat this process with all the other colours to make as many flowers as you need, creating a few spares in case of any breakages. Using a palette knife, transfer them onto your non-stick icing sheet to set overnight.

4 Lightly dust your work surface with icing (powdered) sugar, and roll out black fondant (sugarpaste) to a thickness of about 2mm (¹⁄₈in). Use your circle cutter to create a black centre for each flower.

5 Apply a small amount of edible glue to the centre of each flower.

6 Secure a black centre in place.

7 Leave the flowers to dry.

8 Using edible glue, stick the gerberas at evenly spaced intervals around your cake tiers. Make a repeating pattern of colours if you wish.

TIP:
FLOWER POWER
Always make a few spare flowers as some may break when positioned on the cake. Any spares could be used to decorate the table around the cake, or put on cupcakes, if you're making them.

Instructions: raised flowers

1 You will need to strengthen your fondant (sugarpaste) to make it fit for modelling – see step 1, page 116. Lightly dust your work surface with icing (powdered) sugar and roll out your choice of fondant (sugarpaste) to approximately 2mm (1/8in) thick. Use your gerbera cutters to create six petals: cut two with the 70mm (2¾in) cutter, two with the 56mm (2¼in) cutter and two with the 45mm (1¾in) cutter.

2 Place one of the large flowers onto your flower foam pad and, using the large end of the ball tool, roll along each petal from the tip to the centre to thin it out – this will cause it to curl upwards.

3 Once you are happy with the petals, place the flower in one of your flower cups. This will help to keep the petals curled up slightly for a more realistic look.

4 Repeat step 2 for the second large flower. Once complete, lay it on top of the first flower in the cup using a dab of water or edible glue to stick them together. Layer them so the petals aren't directly on top of one another and the tips of the petals don't touch. Use your ball tool to curl the petals of the two medium-sized flowers, then use some edible glue to secure these in place on top of the two larger petals.

5 To create a really fine finish on your two smallest flowers, snip into the ends of the petals with sharp scissors.

6 Use your ball tool to curl the petals of the smallest flowers upwards. Be careful when you use your ball tool as the petals will now be very delicate.

7 Glue the two smallest flowers in place; you may need to tease the petal tips into shape.

8 Roll a 1cm (½in) ball of black fondant (sugarpaste). Squash it slightly and use edible glue to stick it into the centre of the flower. Use a cocktail stick to gently make small indents in it to make it look like a flower centre. Create as many flowers as required and leave to dry overnight. When you are ready, stick them to your cake with edible glue. You could prop them up on small balls of white fondant (sugarpaste), if you prefer the angle.

TIP:
PUTTING IT ALL TOGETHER
You may want to wait until the cake is in your venue before positioning any of the flowers, as they could fall off or get damaged in the transportation process.

AFTER THE HONEYMOON

So you made your big day truly handmade and personal – hopefully you enjoyed every minute and wished it hadn't gone by so quickly. You spent lots of time creating your perfect day, but you're not quite finished yet – you need to thank your guests for their attendance, good wishes and gifts, and maybe give out copies of your wedding photographs to people.

SAYING THANK YOU

After such a big event, you may well be exhausted from all the planning, organising and crafting – and believe me, that's completely normal. It may be that the last thing you want to do is more crafting, especially if your creative juices have run dry and you'd rather just sleep for the next month! However, it's really important to send out thank you messages to your guests promptly, to reminisce over what a wonderful day you had, and to thank them for being part of it.

Thank you cards

I made really simple thank you cards. I made them to the same size as our save the date cards, so that they fitted in the same envelopes. The only difference was that they were folded, so that we could write a message inside to each guest. By this point in time, we had seen all of our beautiful professional wedding photographs: each time we looked at them, we felt like we were living the day all over again. There was one picture that we both particularly loved, which summed up our joy and elation at finally being married, and at having the perfect weather for it, too. We used that picture as the cover of our cards, and nothing else. We wrote each guest a personal note inside detailing what we had received from them and how grateful we were. Some of our guests have actually framed their cards, probably because I kept the design simple and didn't add any other embellishments or text across the front.

CD case

If you chose a wedding photography package that included a disc of digital images, it could be a nice idea to create copies for your families and for people that were important figures on the day. I made copies for our parents, brothers and sisters, as well as for several of the bridesmaids and groomsmen. I felt it was a small gift in return for all their help, and I knew that they would enjoy some lovely shots of themselves and their families from the day.

Copying the disc is quite straightforward, and I won't go into detail about that here, but you might like to jazz up the CD a little with a cover that indicates what is on the disc. I bought some round CD cases from my local discount store and used the piece of paper inside each case as a template to make my own. I drew a circle onscreen, the same size as the template, including the central circle where the spindle sits; this would later be cut out. I then placed the same image as I used for the thank you cards inside that circle. I used some of the fonts and embellishments from the original invitations to add our names and wedding date onto it. This way, it linked in with all our other wedding stationery.

You could make your own cover using the template, right: simply print out your favourite image the required number of times, and cut each into the correct size circle, using the template as a guide.

SELLING

Even if you did budget and cut costs carefully, there may still be areas where you can recoup some of your money after the big day. All those crafts you made for your ceremony and reception could be sold on to another couple to use at their wedding. Bought items such as vases from your centrepieces or glass jars and candy scoops from your sweet stall could also be sold on. If you're anything like me, such items will end up sitting around your home gathering dust unless you find a specific use for them, so why not have a clear out and start your marriage afresh? Some brides even sell their wedding dress and accessories. I haven't done that yet, but it would be a fabulous way to reclaim some of that money.

I was left with 300m (984½ft) of bunting that I actually felt quite attached to as I had chosen the fabric, my mum had spent hours making it and I had seen it in its full glory. But I had to be realistic and ask myself when, honestly, was I ever going to use the full length again? In the end I decided to keep half and sell half. I managed to get a reasonable price for it on a social media website dedicated to wedding planning in my local area (for more information, see tip box, right). If you can't find one of these near you, try selling via the well-known auction websites, take your goods along to local boot fairs, or hold a garage sale. Try not to get too emotionally attached to everything, although I know that's easier said than done after you've spent months on the planning and making!

TIP:
SWAP IT!

Have a look and see if you can find an online wedding swap shop in your local area. Type in your location, followed by 'wedding swap shop'. It is a bit like using an auction site, but usually you have to request to join the group. Once accepted, you post pictures, details and the price you are hoping to get for your items, and people will comment on those items with a price they are willing to pay. It is generally organised so that you will either deliver the items to that person or they will collect so that there are no shipping costs or packing and delivery worries.

I hope you have enjoyed your journey through my wedding and that you have found some help throughout this book to support you through your big plans.
Good luck and enjoy married life!

TEMPLATES

All the templates are given at actual size.

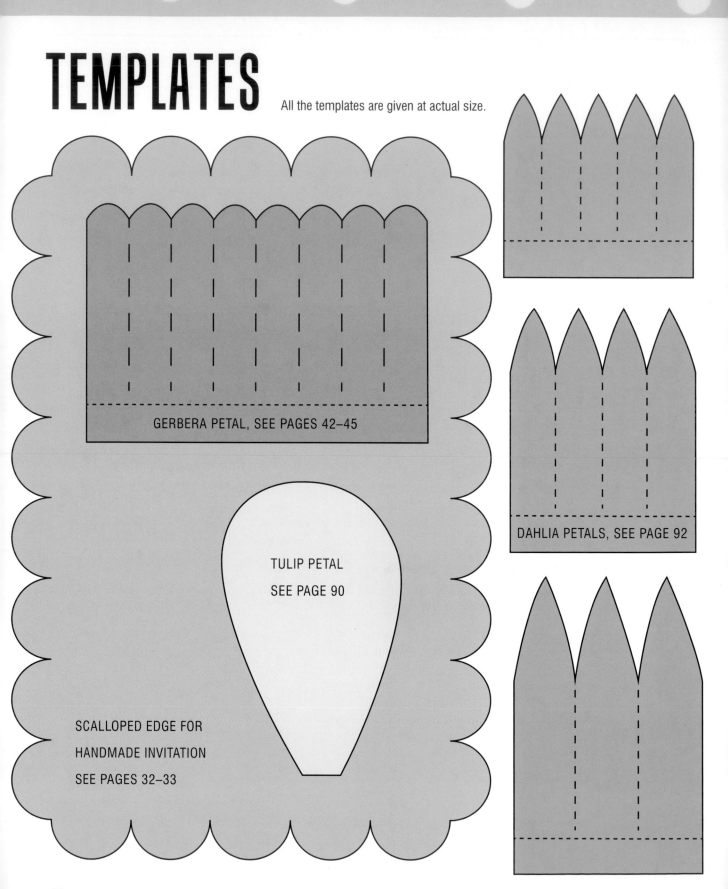

GERBERA PETAL, SEE PAGES 42–45

TULIP PETAL

SEE PAGE 90

SCALLOPED EDGE FOR

HANDMADE INVITATION

SEE PAGES 32–33

DAHLIA PETALS, SEE PAGE 92

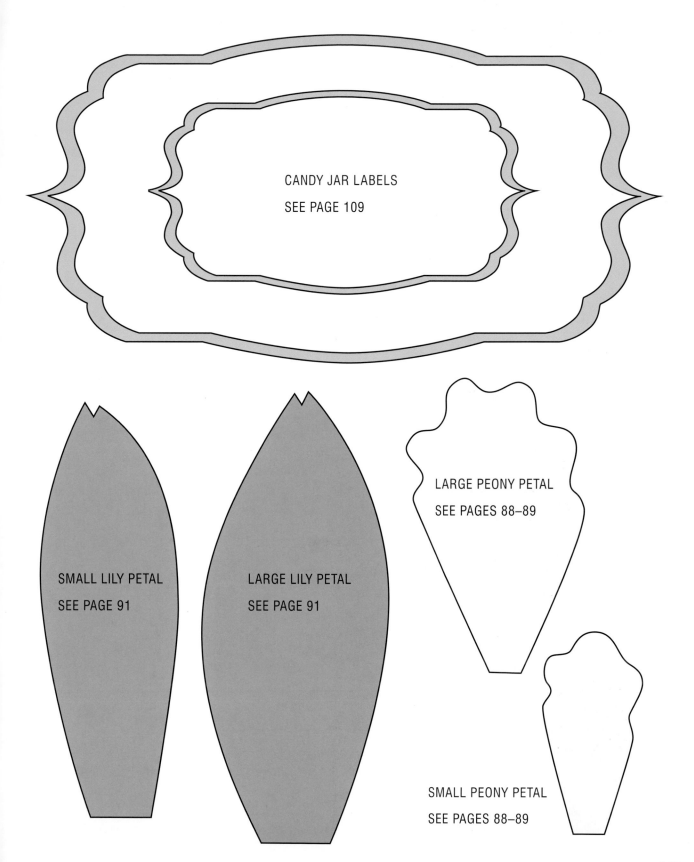

CANDY JAR LABELS

SEE PAGE 109

SMALL LILY PETAL

SEE PAGE 91

LARGE LILY PETAL

SEE PAGE 91

LARGE PEONY PETAL

SEE PAGES 88–89

SMALL PEONY PETAL

SEE PAGES 88–89

TEMPLATES

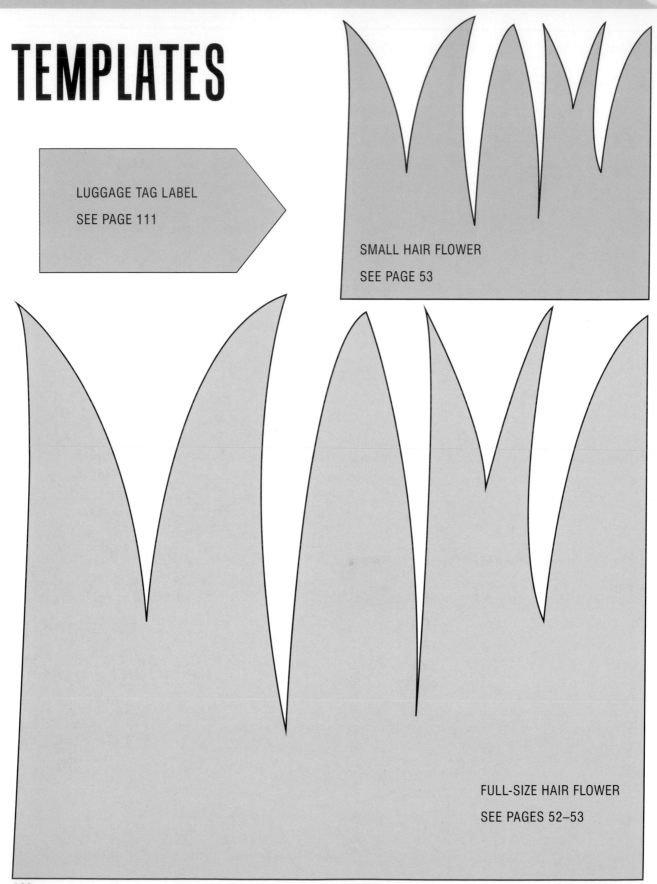

LUGGAGE TAG LABEL

SEE PAGE 111

SMALL HAIR FLOWER

SEE PAGE 53

FULL-SIZE HAIR FLOWER

SEE PAGES 52–53

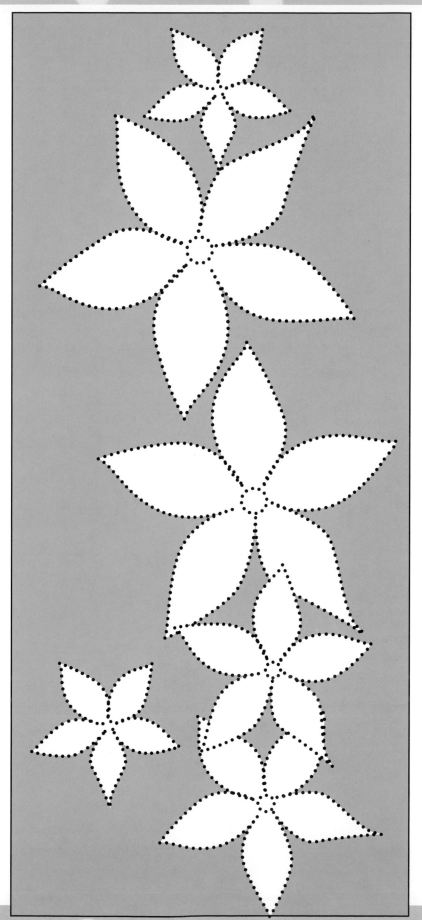

INDEX

ACKNOWLEDGEMENTS

I would like to thank all my friends and family for their help during our wedding planning, creation, set-up and dismantling. Especially: David Miall, Linda and John Mercer, Alison and Chris Miall, Catherine Parsons, Ellie Bristow, Sam Green, Andrea and Neil Underhill, Rachel Buckenham, Richard and Anna Hawthorn, Ben Holmes, Sarah and Mark Crichton, Penny Cooper, Vanessa Ware, Jenny Ware, Chris Rose and Donna Cuthbertson.

A special thank you also needs to go to our suppliers, our vicar Lionel Kevis, the verger Michael Doggett, our photographer Steve Fuller, James McDougall from All American Wedding Cars, Bill Coulstock from Leigh Village Hall, our organist Marilyn Rogowski, Gary and Neil Frost from the band More T Vicar, Nigel Stokes, our caterer and bar manager, my make-up artist Karen Sochon, my hair stylist Nicoll Moss, Ambassador furniture hire, Pantiles Bride and The Cad and Dandy tailors.

I must also thank Becky Shackleton for putting this book together and making some sense out of my scribbles – I have no idea how you managed it!